Pillow Talk
Written and published by J. Parker
© 2019 HHH Books

All scripture quotations, unless otherwise indicated, are taken from The Holy Bible, New International Version®, NIV®, copyright ©1973, 1978, 1984, 2011 by Biblica, Inc.™ Used by permission of Zondervan. All rights reserved worldwide. Scripture quotations marked (NLT) are taken from the Holy Bible, New Living Translation, copyright ©1996, 2004, 2015 by Tyndale House Foundation. Used by permission of Tyndale House Publishers, Inc., Carol Stream, Illinois 60188. All rights reserved. Scripture quotations marked (HCSB) have been taken from the Holman Christian Standard Bible®, Copyright © 1999, 2000, 20002, 2003, 2009 by Holman Bible Publishers. Used by permission. Scripture quotations marked (ESV) are from The ESV® Bible (The Holy Bible, English Standard Version®), copyright © 2001 by Crossway, a publishing ministry of Good News Publishers. Used by permission. All rights reserved.

Cover design by Melinda VanLone at Book Cover Corner
ISBN-13: 978-0-9912542-0-0
ISBN-10: 0-9912542-0-1

Parker, J.
Pillow Talk / J. Parker — 1st ed.

To my Facebook communities, who have asked great questions, given wonderful advice, and helped me determine the topics for this book. May God bless your marriages!

PILLOW TALK

40 Conversations About Sex for Married Couples

J. Parker

HHH Books

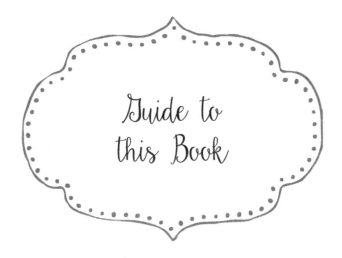

Guide to
this Book

When you were dating, conversing with each other probably wasn't difficult. One of you might have been more reserved and the other more talkative, but most conversations felt natural, productive, connecting. If anything, the comfort level you felt in discussing your history, your daily life, and your goals and dreams signaled that this person was The One—someone you could stay with for the rest of your lives.

But then you entered marriage, and sexual intimacy became a topic you needed to discuss. Maybe you realized how the movies lied about sexual satisfaction just falling into place and it required more coordination. Maybe your personal histories and unspoken expectations made you view the importance, frequency, and activities in your marriage bed differently. Maybe you experienced a good season of sexual intimacy, but then child-rearing, physical struggles, or triggered memories of abuse brought new challenges. Maybe you merely wanted to expand your sexual repertoire, but didn't know how to broach the subject.

Wherever you are in your marriage, ignoring your bedroom issues doesn't make them away. You need to be able to discuss sexual intimacy with respect and honesty.

That's where this book comes in.

Pillow Talk will first walk you through *how* to start those conversations. Whether the topics you want to address are lighthearted or difficult, you'll learn specific tips to set yourselves up for success.

The core of *Pillow Talk* outlines 40 conversations to have with your spouse on a range of issues related to the marriage bed. Each chapter includes questions, relevant scripture, a prayer, and action items to put into practice what you've learned.

The final chapters cover more extreme problems—such as physical inability to perform, sexual abuse in one's past, the damage of pornography—and provide perspective and resources to tackle them. As you move through the conversations, if you uncover one of the extreme issues covered in the final chapters, you may want to pause your progress there and focus instead on the larger issue impeding your sexual intimacy. When sufficient healing has occurred, you can return to the conversations as a couple, without the heartbreaking weight of those wounds.

Must you complete the chapters in order? Not really. The first few chapters lay a good foundation for discussing your marriage bed as a whole, but each chapter is complete on its own. If you choose to jump around, just make sure to cover all the topics at one time or another.

It's not only important, but imperative to your marriage to have the sexual intimacy God designed for you to have. Sex both expresses and nurtures the special connection God intended spouses to share. But embracing God's gift of sex in marriage often begins with a conversation.

Let's get started.

Ground Rules

Whatever you do, don't skip this chapter. Because the success of every conversation in this book relies on your ability to communicate respectfully and effectively with one another.

While discussing sensitive subjects can help us connect with one another in ways that deepen every kind of intimacy in our marriage—mental, emotional, sexual, and spiritual—there is potential for these discussions to backfire, leading to emotional hurt and conflict. Without guidelines, you might find yourselves misreading one another, feeling tense or misunderstood, breaking into arguments.

Each conversation in this book consists of five sections:

Introduction—a single paragraph introducing the topic.

Ask and Listen—three questions to ask of your spouse and then listen to their answers.

Read and Consider—scripture to read together and thoughts on that passage.

Touch and Pray—an invitation to hold hands or embrace and pray over what you've discussed and learned.

Go and Do—two activity options to help you apply what you've learned.

The greatest opportunity for misunderstanding or upset will likely be with section two in which you are tasked to ask one another questions and then listen to your spouse's answers. It's imperative that you do just that. So let's lay some ground rules.

First choose a good time and place.

Have you ever tried to discuss your child's life goals while he's slumped on the living room couch playing a video game? How about asking your boss for a raise as she's running out the door? We can immediately see why such setups would not yield good results. Yet we sometimes fail to set the right atmosphere for important marriage conversations and then act surprised that nothing, or bad things, came of them.

If your marriage bed is currently a place of frustration, get away from the bedroom. Instead, meet in your living room, a secluded area in a nearby park, a corner table at a restaurant, or a neighborhood sidewalk as you stroll together. Find a location that is neutral or—better yet—positive for both of you. Also make sure it's a place where you won't be unnecessarily interrupted. If you do meet in your bedroom, lock the door.

Set aside time and do your best to find which part of the day or week is most likely to result in calm conversation. Attempting to discuss problems when one of you is stressed or weary or angry won't lead to effective listening and problem-solving. If you start the conversation, and you can tell it's not going well due to timing, be willing to reschedule. When it's your turn to answer.

Be honest and vulnerable.

It's tough to share what you really think and feel, even with your spouse. It's a risk to share our hearts with another. We worry that if they knew exactly what went on inside us or in our past, maybe they would view us differently. Yet there is no great gain in intimacy without vulnerability and authenticity.

Be honest first with yourself and with God, and then open up to your spouse. Yes, there may be some emotional pain in doing so and you might get some negative reactions at first, but couple after couple has discovered that their love is greater than their weaknesses. Being fully known and loved is a beautiful, precious gift in marriage—one you should strive to have and to offer. It all begins with honesty (see Colossians 3:9-10).

Consider how you express your concerns.

Even so, we have an obligation to watch our words. Proverbs 12:18 says, "Rash words are like sword thrusts, but the tongue of the wise brings healing" (NRSV). Talking to your spouse should not feel to them like getting poked in the ribs with a rapier. Tell the truth, but watch how you phrase your message.

As an example, let's say you want more frequent sex. You aren't likely to have a great conversation with statements like:

"There's something wrong that you don't want sex more." [Translation: There's something wrong with YOU.]

"I'm a man! I need to have sex more!" [Translation: It's not about intimacy, just a physical need.]

"If I'd known you didn't want sex, I wouldn't have married you." [Translation: I don't really love you; it's just about the sex.]

Maybe you'd get some duty sex, but blaming or demands don't work in the long-term and instead build resentment for one spouse and dissatisfaction for the other.

Rather than aiming to be acknowledged as right, aim for being understood. Focus on your perspective, your feelings, and your desires regarding sexual intimacy, rather than "getting it off your chest" or listing perceived offenses. Concentrate on how you and your spouse can address problems together and grow in your sexual intimacy.

Keep your requests reasonable.

If you've been having sex once a month and you expect to start having it every day, you need to dial back your expectations. Yes, you may feel like you're in a sexual desert and a spoonful of intimacy isn't nearly enough. However, change takes time. Prioritize moving in the right direction, and over time you can make a lot of progress.

Also celebrate progress you've made through the years and small successes you achieve as you go through *Pillow Talk*. Being married has the distinct advantage of allowing a long period in which to make huge strides in fostering intimacy—but they're made step by step.

When it's your spouse's turn to answer.

Listen.

Do not interrupt, do not correct, do not contradict, do not defend, do not criticize. Whether you agree with or understand your spouse's responses, validate their feelings by listening and believing what they say. Even if your spouse is wrong about something, showing respect and acceptance creates a safe space for your spouse to reveal themselves more fully to you.

We are far more willing to open up to people when we believe we won't be judged, insulted, or dismissed for our thoughts and feelings. Feeling accepted and cherished also leads to more openness to sex. So it's in your interest to listen carefully, respectfully, and lovingly to your spouse when it's their turn to speak.

Stay calm.

This may not be easy at times. If you experience physiological changes signaling sadness, fear, or anger—such as blood rushing to your head, pounding of your heart, tension in your muscles—make an effort to calm yourself. That may involve one or more of the following:

Deep breathing, a meditation technique demonstrated to calm our bodies. Breathe in slowly through your nose, then out of your mouth several times, until your breathing returns to normal.

Meditative prayer; that is, memorizing a scripture to recite when you find yourself becoming upset. See, for example, Psalm 56:3, Proverbs 10:12, Luke 6:31, Philippians 4:13, 1 Peter 5:7, 1 John 4:11.

Touching your spouse—wrapping your arm around them, holding their hand, or putting your hand on their arm or leg. Extended touching can release the body chemicals serotonin and oxytocin, which have calming and bonding effects.

Asking for a break from the conversation, with a definite time that you will return, cooler-headed and ready to proceed.

Seek clarification.

Once your spouse has answered the question completely, if you take issue with something they said, ask for clarification. Without getting defensive or critical, repeat back what you think you heard and ask them to confirm or clarify.

If you have follow-up questions, go ahead and ask. Use this opportunity to learn as much as possible about how your spouse views the topic.

Accept their feelings.

One of the worst things to say is "You shouldn't feel like that." Feelings just happen. They can be based on truths or errors or lies, but feelings themselves won't simply leave by willing them away. So stop arguing about how the other feels. Instead, tackle why they feel that way.

Your spouse's feelings about sex make complete sense—given their underlying beliefs. For instance, if your wife has experienced sexual trauma in the past at the hands of men and you're constantly talking about wanting her to give you sex, it makes sense for her to feel used and unvalued; or if your husband has been rebuffed by you a million times with excuses of how busy you are, it makes sense for him to feel disrespected and unwanted. Simply respect that your spouse doesn't see the world, your marriage, and your marriage bed the same way you do.

Think through their answers.

If you spouse shared their heart with you, honor that by letting their words sink in, mulling over where they're coming from, acknowledging where they made good points and how you can address them, and responding to their reasonable requests.

When Jesus prays that God will bring us into complete unity (John 17:23), He is talking about our mutual bonding to Christ, not matching each other in every regard. Let the variety of God's beautiful creation be seen in your spouse, seeking unity where it really matters—in your commitment to Christ and to your marriage.

Now on to the conversations.

Pillow Talk

Chapter 1
PRAYING ABOUT OUR SEX LIFE

Perhaps you prayed before marriage about avoiding sexual sin and maintaining purity. Perhaps you continue to pray such prayers. But what about inviting God into your marriage bed? What about talking to Him directly about what you desire, where you struggle, and any disunity you have in your marriage? What about inviting Him to bless your sexual intimacy?

Ask and Listen

1. Have you ever prayed about our sex life? If so, what have you prayed?

2. Are you comfortable praying with me about our sexual intimacy? Why or why not?

3. How would you like us to pray about our marriage bed?

Read and Consider

Read together Philippians 4:5-7.

Let your gentleness be evident to all. The Lord is near. Do not be anxious about anything, but in every situation, by prayer and petition, with thanksgiving, present your requests to God. And the peace of God, which transcends all understanding, will guard your hearts and your minds in Christ Jesus.

Notice those words *anything* and *in every situation*? There are no restrictions about what we can bring before God. He's open to hearing it all. If we are anxious about something, He wants to know. If we have a request, He longs to listen. If we are thankful, He appreciates our gratitude.

Our bedroom is not off-limits, but rather another area where God wants us to thrive according to His plan. He created sex and wants it to bless our marriages. That means we can bring this topic before God—as individuals or together—and pour our hearts out to Him.

In the process of praying, we will find the comfort of God's presence and, if we are open to Him, changes to our own hearts and perspectives. When we talk to God and then listen, we often find His answer to our prayer is molding us to become more committed and better equipped to pursue healthy and holy sexual intimacy. He grants wisdom, perseverance, and love.

Touch and Pray

*Dear Lord, even though we know You created
sex, and that You see and know everything, the
private and sensitive nature of sex can make it feel
awkward for us to speak up before You and each
other. Please settle our nerves, open our hearts, and
give our thoughts and desires the right words.*

*[Pray for any specific concerns you
mentioned in your discussion.]*

In the name of Christ, Amen.

Go and Do

1. Write a prayer about your sexual intimacy, telling God about your struggles, your fears, your longings, your joys. If you want to share it with your spouse, you may. Or you can keep it to yourself, refer back to the prayer, and pray it again the next day or week or however often you wish.

2. Hold hands with your spouse or embrace and pray together about your marriage bed. One of you can say the whole prayer or you can take turns, but make sure both spouses' concerns are addressed. This exercise may feel awkward at first, but continue it for seven days. Then share how these prayers have affected you.

Pillow Talk

Chapter 2
WHAT WE LEARNED ABOUT SEX

How we grew up hearing and thinking about sex can make a big imprint on our perspective later in life. Unfortunately, few Christians report having received thorough, positive, Scripture-based instruction about sexuality. How has what you learned impacted your sexual intimacy?

Ask and Listen

1. What's your earliest memory of sex? When did you learn about it, and what did you learn?

2. What messages about sex did you get from your parents, mentors, and the church as you grew up?

3. What, if anything, that you learned about sex as a child has negatively affected your view of physical intimacy now?

Read and Consider

Read together Deuteronomy 6:6-9.

> *These commandments that I give you today are to*
> *be on your hearts. Impress them on your children.*
> *Talk about them when you sit at home and when*
> *you walk along the road, when you lie down and*
> *when you get up. Tie them as symbols on your hands*
> *and bind them on your foreheads. Write them on*
> *the doorframes of your houses and on your gates.*

God's pronouncement to the Israelites in this passage involved teaching the children who God was, what He had done for His people, and how they should honor Him by living according to His commands. This foundational education was to be an ongoing practice, saturating their daily existence.

Within the law of Moses, they were expected to follow commands about sex which showed God's desire for it to remain holy and mutually satisfying in marriage. But many of us weren't taught what God's design for sex really was. Instead, our parents and church leaders were silent, ignorant, or negative. Often they hadn't received godly instruction themselves and didn't know how to teach us.

It's not too late to learn. God's Word can still teach you what it means to experience intimate, meaningful, and pleasurable sex as God intended in the covenant bond of marriage.

Touch and Pray

Holy Father, You are the creator of sex, the designer of pleasure and intimacy in the marriage bed. But we have struggled with messages that make it difficult for us to fully embrace the gift You long for us to enjoy. Help us to align our understanding with Yours.

[Pray specifically for the issues you brought up in your conversation.]

In Jesus' blessed name, Amen.

Do and Do

1. Take a sheet of paper and make two columns. On the left side, write down underlying messages about sex that you got from the teaching you received. Those can be anything from "sex is good in marriage" to "only bad girls want sex" or "sex is for the man." In the right-hand column, counter any negative messages with your growing understanding of what God says about sexual intimacy. You don't have to believe these yet, but record what you think is the right answer. Finally, put a star by those erroneous messages you struggle with most.

2. Trade lists. Yes, this is a vulnerable exercise. But let your spouse see where you're struggling, so they can help and pray for you. In turn, promise to help and pray for your spouse.

Pillow Talk

Chapter 3
STAYING SEXUALLY HEALTHY

While sexual intimacy in marriage involves more than our bodies—our minds, hearts, and souls—our bodies need to be in proper shape to function during foreplay and intercourse. That doesn't mean we must be a particular weight or athletic, merely that our bodies should be able to experience arousal, pleasure, and climax. When something goes awry, it's time to seek answers.

Ask and Listen

1. What obstacles do you feel like your body presents for experiencing arousal, pleasure, and/or climax?

2. What, if any, health concerns do you have about my body's responses to sex?

3. What steps do you think we should take to pursue better physical health and thus better sexual intimacy?

Read and Consider

Read together 1 Timothy 4:8 and 3 John 1:2.

For physical training is of some value, but godliness has value for all things, holding promise for both the present life and the life to come.

Dear friend, I pray that you may enjoy good health and that all may go well with you, even as your soul is getting along well.

Both the apostle Paul and the apostle John stress the importance of health. Yes, of course, they believed—as we should—that the higher goal was godliness, but they still spoke directly to friends (Timothy and Gaius) about physical training and good health.

God has also shown many times in Scripture that He desires good health for His people—including warnings against gluttony and drunkenness, instructions in Leviticus regarding proper care of diseases and infections, and the miracles of healing that Jesus performed.

In our broken world, our bodies sometimes don't function as well as they should. If you're experiencing painful intercourse, erectile dysfunction, hormonal deficiencies, or any health issues that get in the way of enjoying sex, you should pursue healing and health as best you can. Do what you can to train your body for pleasurable and satisfying intimacy in your marriage bed.

Touch and Pray

Lord, You are the healer of our souls. We pray also that You will strengthen and heal our bodies, so that we can pursue sexual intimacy in our marriage. Empower us to the steps we need to take to properly care for our bodies and address physical obstacles we experience.

[Pray for the health concerns you each have.]

In the name of our Great Physician Jesus, Amen.

Go and Do

1. Schedule a routine physical or well-woman exam with your doctor, or a sexual health specialist if you're experiencing severe problems. Ask to have a physical exam of your sexual organs, to get your hormonal levels checked, and to attain referrals for any specialty appointments you may need. Possible screenings include Pap Smears and mammograms for women, prostate cancer screenings for men, and colonoscopies for both genders. And keep that appointment.

2. Consider where you should make lifestyle changes that will facilitate healthier and more enjoyable sex. For instance, regular exercise increases flexibility, mood, libido, and body confidence. Overeating, especially heavy carbohydrate foods, too much alcohol, and smoking have a detrimental effect on sexual health. Take stock, choose a

few baby steps to start you in the right direction, and then take that first one.

Chapter 4
PREPARING OUR BEDROOM

Imagine the perfect bedroom in which to make love. Now compare that to your actual bedroom. Those two images are likely not the same, and in some cases wildly dissimilar. While we have to live in the real world, where daily life and its constraints keep us from achieving the dream, we should strive to make our bedroom a place where we want to go. A place that's conducive to making love.

Ask and Listen

1. What aspects of our bedroom make it difficult for us to prioritize making love? (For example, television, mess, etc.)

2. What could we change to help our bedroom become a better place to connect?

3. Given our time, money, and circumstances, what can we do right now?

Read and Consider

Read together Song of Songs 1:16-17.

She: *How handsome you are, my beloved!*

Oh, how charming!

And our bed is verdant.

He: *The beams of our house are cedars;*

our rafters are firs.

The phrasing here makes us think this couple was making love outside, with the verdant green beneath them and trees above. Regardless, this is a peaceful place for them to be together. They look forward to making love there.

Unfortunately, if we wrote that poem, it might read, "How handsome you are, you sexy thang! Oh, how charming! But our bed is an absolute mess. The TV in our bedroom is booming, and our laundry piles are looming." Not exactly the best setting for lovemaking.

Take some time and effort to make your bedroom your own pleasure paradise—an inviting location that encourages you both to engage in physical intimacy.

Touch and Pray

Dear God, we thank You for the roof over our heads, the bedroom where we sleep and make love, and the many other ways You have met our needs. Help us to create an atmosphere where marriage is honored and intimacy pursued.

[Pray for specific needs, such as time, finances, unity, etc.]

In the name of our Savior, Amen.

Go and Do

1.   Create a "vision board" or inspiration collage with your spouse. Each of you can add pictures, samples, and thoughts about your ideal bedroom. While you may never achieve all that you long to have, this can help you see what's important to both of you, grow closer as you dream together, and come up with ideas you actually can implement.

2.   List the ideas you discussed with your spouse (#3 in Ask and Listen above). Then make them happen, or plan when and how they will happen.

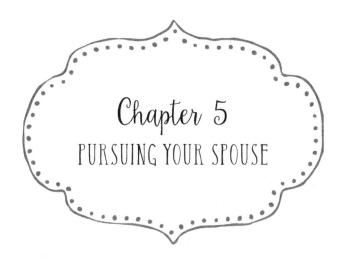

Chapter 5
PURSUING YOUR SPOUSE

The rock band Cheap Trick sang, "I want you to want me." We can all relate to these simple lyrics, that longing to be desired. When you first met or began dating or got married, you likely pursued one another in ways that demonstrated that you genuinely wanted to be with your spouse. But once we get into marriage, we sometimes forget how important it is to make that clear—even when it comes to the marriage bed.

Ask and Listen

1. Tell me about a time when you felt I really desired you and how it made you feel.

2. Do you think I pursue you enough now in our marriage? Why or why not?

3. How could I better show that I desire all of you, including sexual intimacy with you?

Read and Consider

Read together 1 John 4:7-12.

> *Dear friends, let us love one another, for love comes from God. Everyone who loves has been born of God and knows God. Whoever does not love does not know God, because God is love. This is how God showed his love among us: He sent his one and only Son into the world that we might live through him. This is love: not that we loved God, but that he loved us and sent his Son as an atoning sacrifice for our sins. Dear friends, since God so loved us, we also ought to love one another. No one has ever seen God; but if we love one another, God lives in us and his love is made complete in us.*

At first glance, this passage may not seem to have anything to say about pursuing one another, although it certainly says a lot about love. Except that we are often told in Scripture to love as Jesus loved. And when we read passages such as 1 John 4:7-12, we see how much Jesus sought us out. Later in verse 19, John confirms this by saying, "We love because he first loved us."

By pursuing one another in love, showing our desire and affection for one another, we are living out Jesus's example in a romantic way in marriage. As our Bridegroom pursued us, His bride, we should pursue our beloved spouse here on earth. So flirt, initiate, and engage with your spouse, showing that you want and value your beloved.

Touch and Pray

*Thank you, Lord, for setting the example for how
we should love—for pursuing us with Your words
and Your actions. Help us to pursue one another
this coming week through words and actions
that speak love in ways we can hear and believe.
Help us to nurture our desire for one another.*

*[Pray for the ability to follow through
with what your spouse asked for.]*

In the name of our Bridegroom Jesus, Amen.

Go and Do

1.   Make a list of five ways you can flirt with your spouse this week. Aim for romance, playfulness, and affirmation. It can be a loving note left on their mirror, a no-strings-attached massage, or whatever else you would both enjoy. But pursue your spouse this week romantically, apart from efforts or expectations for sex.

2.   It can be especially difficult for the lower-drive spouse to be the pursuer regarding sexual intimacy. But if you are the lower-drive spouse, make an effort this week to show sexual interest. Yes, you may worry this will simply egg them on, and it can feel awkward, but odds are that it will be well-received and even stir your own libido. If you're the

higher-drive spouse, let your lower-drive honey take the lead and show appreciation for their efforts.

Chapter 6
OUR BODY AND SELF IMAGE

If you could look like anyone, who would you look like? Too few of us would answer that question "myself." We are all too aware of physical flaws, real or imagined, and fail to appreciate our unique appeal. Yet self-criticism or lack of confidence about your appearance can prevent you from enjoying sexual intimacy and/or sharing your body with your spouse. Let's tackle wrong messages we've adopted about our bodies and ourselves.

Ask and Listen

1. What messages did you receive about your body growing up?

2. How do you feel about your body now? What do you like and/or not like about it?

3. What could I do to make you feel better about your body?

Read and Consider

Read together Psalm 139:13-15.

For you created my inmost being;
you knit me together in my mother's womb.

I praise you because I am fearfully and won-
derfully made; your works are wonderful,

I know that full well.

My frame was not hidden from you when
I was made in the secret place, when I was
woven together in the depths of the earth.

Even though we know that we were fashioned by an amazing Creator, we often struggle with how we feel about our bodies. We experience negative messages or encounter unrealistic standards for beauty or strength. We compare ourselves to models with hourglass figures or actors with muscular six-packs and know we don't measure up. We secretly think the most attractive people are also the sexiest, and if we aren't them, what does that mean about our appeal in the marriage bed?

However, most spouses are content with their lover's body. When that's not happening, it's usually because (1) the spouse has selfish, unrealistic expectations and/or (2) the lover has neglected their grooming or health to the extreme. But those are far ends of the continuum, and most of the time our spouse is much happier with our body than we are.

If your spouse is excited to engage with you, and God Himself approves of His handiwork, shouldn't you strive to embrace your body fully? We are indeed "fearfully and wonderfully made."

Touch and Pray

> *Lord, You made us in Your image, and we insult what You've created when we are overly critical of our appearance. Help us instead to see the wonder and beauty of our bodies, with all of their intricacies, with distinct masculine and feminine traits, and with the ability to provide pleasure to one another in the marriage bed.*
>
> *[Pray specifically for the challenges you each have with body and self image.]*
>
> *We praise You for Your handiwork. In Jesus' name, Amen.*

Go and Do

1. List three things you like about your body—big or small—and make a point to pay attention to those positive attributes when you look in the mirror over the coming week.

2. If you have neglected your health or grooming, sketch out a plan for how you'll address that issue. For instance, set up an exercise plan you can engage in as a couple, shop together for more flattering clothes and lingerie, schedule a back-waxing, etc.

Chapter 7
THE ROLE OF FRIENDSHIP

When spouses feel distant or uninterested in sexual intimacy, one key component could be a lack of friendship. It's important to know and feel that your beloved cares not only for your body or the roles you perform in your family, but for you as a person. From a place of close friendship, we can become more generous and loving in the marriage bed.

Ask and Listen

1. What traits do you look for in a friend?
2. Do you think of me as one of your closest friends? Why or why not?[1]
3. What specific steps could we take to deepen our friendship?

---

[1]More men than women name their spouse as their "best friend." But that may indicate nothing more than the number of friends from which we have to choose and how we each define "best friend." See Curtin, Melanie. "Spouses Who Have This 1 View of Their Partner Are Twice as Happy in Life." Inc.com. March 21, 2018. Accessed September 07, 2018. https://www.inc.com/melanie-curtin/spouses-who-view-their-partners-in-this-1-specific-way-are-twice-as-satisfied-in-life.html.

Read and Consider

Read together Song of Songs 5:16.

His mouth is sweetness itself;
he is altogether lovely.
This is my beloved, this is my friend,
daughters of Jerusalem.

Right at the end of a wife's listing of what she adores
about her husband's body is this proclamation: her husband
is also her friend. She happily lets her other friends—daughters of Jerusalem—know that her lover is close to her in
other ways.

Sex within marriage should be the culmination of so
many attachments to one another: romantic, friendly, passionate, and intimate. It's a shared-life experience.

Touch and Pray

Dear God, although You are our Lord and
Savior, Jesus also called us His friends (John
15:15). We thank You for this friendship with
Christ and with one another. Help us in our
marriage to build the commitment, joy, and
trust that characterize lifelong friends.

[Pray for God's help in taking the steps you
discussed to nurture your friendship.]

In the name of our friend Jesus, Amen.

•)(•

Go and Do

1. Write down five personality or character traits that make your spouse a good friend. Share your lists with one another, explaining in more detail what you appreciate about each other's friendship.

2. Sit down together and make a list of activities you have enjoyed doing together, currently or in the past. Add any activities you're interested in trying together. Discuss how you can practically build those together times into your calendar.

Pillow Talk

Chapter 8
YOU THINK YOU KNOW ME

When you first got together, you likely spent a lot of time getting to know one another. You asked questions, listened carefully, and pursued interests and activities that helped you learn more about your beloved. But years or decades into marriage, you may think you know most of what there is to know—even if you still don't understand exactly what's happening in your spouse's brain. But how well do you really know each other, especially when it comes to sex?

Ask and Listen

1. When it comes to our sex life, what assumptions do you think I've made about you that are untrue?

2. What do you wish I understood more fully about your sexuality?

3. How can I better understand what you're thinking and feeling in the moment?

Read and Consider

Read together Proverbs 18:2.

Fools find no pleasure in understanding, but
delight in airing their own opinions.

No one wants to be called a fool, but if we're honest with ourselves, this is what happens when we make assumptions. We delight in believing that we know what's really going on with our spouse, that we have the answers for why they behave the way they do. We may make the calculation that if we did ABC, it would mean XYZ. But our spouse is different person with different motivations and feelings and sensitivities—uniquely made by God.

This verse instead encourages us to take pleasure in understanding, to ask our spouse what's going on and sympathize with their perspective. When we become willing to listen to our spouse, to study them more carefully, to put ourselves in their shoes, then we can begin to address where we are in our marriage bed. And how to get where we want to be.

Touch and Pray

*Our Creator, You have made us such intricate
beings, with layers and layers of complexity. Help
us to never forget the wonder of all that went into
creating our beloved and who they are today. Give
us a desire to keep learning about one another, to
ask questions that help us gain understanding, to
study their ways, and to respect our differences.*

[Pray for any particulars you need to work on.]

We praise You in the name of Your Son Jesus, Amen.

Do and Do

1. Take the "How Well Do You Know Your Spouse?" quiz
at Appendix A, then trade quiz sheets and talk about your
answers. Were there any surprises? What might this tell you
about how well you know your spouse's preferences?

2. Practice active listening with the following exercise.
Choose which spouse will go first. Have that person take
five minutes to tell a story (from your childhood, a recent
workplace incident, a memory from when you were dating, whatever). When the five minutes are up, the listening
spouse should repeat back what they heard and ask clarifying
questions. Take turns, and see how much more insight into
your spouse you can gain.

Pillow Talk

Chapter 9
ARE YOU IN THE MOOD?

Many spouses think lovemaking should happen when they're "in the mood." Yet our feelings and desires can be fickle, and we can misunderstand our spouse's feelings and desires and thus miss opportunities to be intimate. Not every sexual encounter must happen with both spouses rarin' to go. Rather, a spouse can initiate, engage, respond, or warm up slowly to the idea.

Ask and Listen

1. What does it mean for you to be "in the mood"?

2. Even if you're not in the mood at the moment, how can I figure out whether you'd be receptive to making love?

3. What are some good ways for me to initiate sex?

Read and Consider

Read together Song of Songs 5:2-6.

I slept but my heart was awake.
Listen! My beloved is knocking:
"Open to me, my sister, my darling,
my dove, my flawless one.
My head is drenched with dew,
my hair with the dampness of the night."
I have taken off my robe—
must I put it on again?
I have washed my feet—
must I soil them again?
My beloved thrust his hand
through the latch-opening;
my heart began to pound for him.
I arose to open for my beloved,
and my hands dripped with myrrh,
my fingers with flowing myrrh,
on the handles of the bolt.
I opened for my beloved,
but my beloved had left; he was gone.
My heart sank at his departure.

Just like the husband and wife in this passage, signals can get crossed. One spouse is ready to make love, but the other isn't there. Or at least, not yet. Our efforts to initiate sex can be clumsy, poorly timed, or misread.

Yet one way or another, you need to be able to get this party started. You need to figure out what types of communication and affection work best for you individually and as a couple.

Even if doing what your spouse desires feels awkward at first, you can form new habits for approaching and arousing your beloved. It's important to talk about what you can reasonably do to help one another get in the mood for lovemaking, so that sex becomes a regular part of your marriage.

Touch and Pray

Dear Lord, sometimes we're just not in the mood to make love. Yet we don't want to miss opportunities to connect physically that would strengthen our marriage and deepen our intimacy. Help us to be sensitive to one another's moods, to ways we can help our spouse get in the mood, and to the best ways to initiate sexual intimacy. Help us also to understand those times when lovemaking doesn't happen, despite one of us desiring it, and to make those instances an uncommon occurrence for our marriage bed.

[Pray for each other's sexual interest and initiation.]

In Jesus' holy name, Amen.

Do and Do

1. Use a green light/red light system this week to indicate when you're open to—not necessarily in the mood, but open to—making love. For instance, put on a candle on each of your nightstands and light it if you're interested, wear a certain item to bed to indicate willingness, or tie a ribbon or cord around your wrist. When you're both "green," that's when one or both of you should initiate.

2. Match your start-up to one of the ways requested by your spouse in your discussion. Follow through with what they asked for, and make sure you show enthusiasm for their approach. If you're the one receiving the initiation, reward the startup with full engagement in the marriage bed. Positive consequences increase the likelihood of repetition.

Chapter 10
HOW OFTEN SHOULD WE MAKE LOVE?

One of the common conflicts about sexual intimacy in marriage is how frequently it should be happening. Spouses tend to answer the question of "how often is enough?" differently, and negotiating frequency can prove a challenge in some marriages.

Ask and Listen

1. If it was entirely up to you, how often would you want to make love?

2. What would having more frequent sexual encounters mean to you?

3. What ideas do you have for working through our differences in sex drive?

Read and Consider

Read together 1 Corinthians 7:3-5.

> *The husband should fulfill his marital duty to his wife, and likewise the wife to her husband. The wife does not have authority over her own body but yields it to her husband. In the same way, the husband does not have authority over his own body but yields it to his wife. Do not deprive each other except perhaps by mutual consent and for a time, so that you may devote yourselves to prayer. Then come together again so that Satan will not tempt you because of your lack of self-control.*

Too often, this passage is used as a plea for lower-drive spouses to give higher-drive spouses more sex. But these verses aren't about demanding what you deserve to have in your marriage or schlepping to the bedroom to fulfill your "marital duty." Rather, the core message is the mutuality of sexual intimacy in marriage. Both husband and wife have an obligation to invest in regular sexual intimacy.

We are to yield to one another, understanding that ours is a one-flesh covenant—our connection so strong that depriving each other is also depriving ourselves and our marriage. The takeaway isn't that one spouse can determine the frequency, and the other must comply. Rather, you should each pursue regular sexual intimacy as you also make every attempt to live in unity.[2]

---

[2] If sex is not happening due to deeper issues with the relationship, sexual abuse in the past, or pornography use, you will need to address those before expecting frequency to increase.

Touch and Pray

Our Heavenly Father, You designed sex for more than childbearing—it is also a unique way for couples to connect and express love. We want to claim the benefits of regular lovemaking in our marriage. Help us to let go of our selfishness in demanding or refusing sex and instead seek unity and intimacy.

[Pray about working through discrepancies in sexual interest or obstacles with time and energy.]

May we honor Your design for sex in marriage. In the name of our Savior, Amen.

Go and Do

1. Make a guess about how many times you make love in the course of a month, then track your frequency for the next 30 days and see how close you are to your estimate. Did you make love more or less than you thought, and what does that say about any changes you need to make?

2. List sexual activities that you'd be up for doing even without intercourse. Then share your lists with one another, so you each know what the other would be fine with if and when intercourse is off the table.

Pillow Talk

Chapter 11
OUR SEXUAL REPERTOIRE

What's on your sexual menu tonight? Sometimes it seems one spouse wants one menu and the other spouse wants a different menu, but with sex being a twosome activity, you have to agree on what menu you'll both order from. Talking about your sexual repertoire outside the bedroom can help you experience greater comfort, confidence, pleasure, and unity inside the bedroom.

Ask and Listen

1. Besides intercourse, what's your favorite sexual activity we do and why?

2. What sexual activity would you like for us to try, at least once, and why?

3. What resources do you think would be good for us to glean godly ideas for our sexual repertoire?

Read and Consider

Read together Song of Songs 7:10-13.

I belong to my beloved,
and his desire is for me.
Come, my beloved, let us
go to the countryside,
let us spend the night in the villages.
Let us go early to the vineyards
to see if the vines have budded,
if their blossoms have opened,
and if the pomegranates are in bloom—
there I will give you my love.
The mandrakes send out their fragrance,
and at our door is every delicacy,
both new and old,
that I have stored up for you, my beloved.

"At our door is every delicacy." That's quite a phrase to describe the lovemaking between husband and wife! Perhaps this indicates the variety of sexual experiences they shared, the sensations they felt, the pleasures they savored.

Although we need to consider whether a desired sexual activity is right or wrong, wise or foolish, many Christians find it surprising how much freedom God has given us in the marriage bed.

We can choose a variety of locations, positions, movements, touches, and actions to arouse and satisfy our lover and ourselves. Not every option available must be embraced, but consider what you might be willing to add to your sexual repertoire. Then come to unity about something new, and potentially exciting, to try.

Touch and Pray

*Our loving Creator, You made sex to be more
than intercourse, but rather a whole feast of
delights for husband and wife to enjoy. Guide
us to knowing which activities we should
include in our marriage bed and which ones
we should exclude. We want to honor You and
each other as we develop our sexual repertoire.*

*[Pray for what you need to do to get on the
same page about your sexual repertoire.]*

We pray in Jesus' name, Amen.

Do and Do

1. Create a sexual menu of activities you'd both like to
try—whether you've done them before or not. Then start
marking off the list in your intimate encounters.

2. After you've tried something new, evaluate how it went.
Do you want to keep it? Do both or one of you want to
put that in the discard pile? It's okay to try something and
decide you don't like it. But often, couples find they enjoyed
the new activity or could tweak it next time to work better.
Revise your sexual menu accordingly.

Pillow Talk

Chapter 12
DESCRIBING OUR INTIMATE PARTS

When you first learned about your sexual body parts, you might have used a childish or euphemistic name to describe them, or perhaps you learned their clinical terms. Later, you might have shifted into using crass words or simply nicknames to refer to these parts. But how we talk about our own bodies and our spouse's body can set a tone for our sexual intimacy.

Ask and Listen

1. How do you refer to your sexual body parts? What names or terms do you use?

2. What words do you wish I would use to describe your sexual parts?

3. What words, terms, or general language do you think should be off-limits in describing one another's body parts?

Read and Consider

Read together Song of Songs 7:6-10.

He: *How beautiful you are and how*
        pleasing, my love, with your delights!

        Your stature is like that of the palm,
        and your breasts like clusters of fruit.

        I said, "I will climb the palm tree;
        I will take hold of its fruit."

        May your breasts be like clusters of
        grapes on the vine, the fragrance of
        your breath like apples, and your
        mouth like the best wine.

She: *May the wine go straight to my beloved,*
        flowing gently over lips and teeth.

        I belong to my beloved,
        and his desire is for me.

Throughout Song of Songs, the husband and wife describe one another's bodies in beautiful yet erotic words. In this passage, the husband expresses admiration of his wife's body, specifically describing the appeal of her bust. As in other passages of this book, there is both metaphor and plain language to name body parts; thus, he refers to both "breasts" and "fruit." And the wife responds to his passionate description with arousal and longing.

While the language is definitely erotic, it's not disrespectful or degrading. If a term feels disrespectful or degrading to your spouse, it should not be used in the marriage bed.

But there are thousands of ways we can erotically express our admiration for our spouse's body. Consider it a challenge to get creative in how you speak to one another in ways that arouse and stir sexual longing.

Touch and Pray

God, You designed every part of our bodies, including our erogenous zones and genitals. Thank You for the beauty and utility of our bodies for making love. Help us to be respectful and admiring in how we talk about one another's bodies. Give us the right words to arouse and satisfy one another.

[Pray for specifics of how you deal with language in your marriage bed.]

In the name of our glorious Savior, Amen.

Do and Do

1. Come up with three words or phrases to refer to your spouse's body parts that you haven't used before. These can be straightforward, poetic, or humorous, but then find some time in your lovemaking to use them and see how your spouse responds. To the receiving spouse: Be open to the new words and give feedback in a positive way, asking your spouse to change words if desired.

2. Lie together naked in bed and take tours of one another's bodies, naming the sights along the way. That is, use your eyes and your hand or a single finger to slowly work your way up or down your spouse's body, stopping here and there to express with erotic language how you feel about these body parts God designed.

Chapter 13
HOW LONG SHOULD SEX TAKE?

Although we might relish the idea of making love all night long, that's not exactly realistic. The average length of a sexual encounter appears to be around twenty minutes (foreplay + intercourse).[3] For couples under time pressures, finding even twenty minutes can seem a daunting goal. But what's more problematic is when you and your spouse don't see eye-to-eye on how long sex should last.

Ask and Listen

1. If we could find the time, how long would you like a sexual encounter to last and why?

2. What challenges do we face in achieving your desired time for a sexual encounter?

---

[3]See Miller, S. Andrea, and E. Sandra Byers. "Actual and Desired Duration of Foreplay and Intercourse: Discordance and Misperceptions within Heterosexual Couples." *The Journal of Sex Research* 41, no. 3 (2004): 301-09. doi:10.1080/00224490409552237; Nkayla Afshariyan For Daily Mail Australia. "Research Reveals How Long Sex Lasts for the Average Person." Daily Mail Online. March 28, 2017. Accessed November 24, 2018. https://www.dailymail.co.uk/femail/article-4358636/Research-reveals-long-sex-lasts-average-person.html.

3. How can we incorporate marathon, mid-length, and quickies into our sexual intimacy?

Read and Consider

Read together Ecclesiastes 3:1-8.

> *There is a time for everything, and a season*
> *for every activity under the heavens:*
> *a time to be born and a time to die,*
> *a time to plant and a time to uproot,*
> *a time to kill and a time to heal,*
> *a time to tear down and a time to build,*
> *a time to weep and a time to laugh,*
> *a time to mourn and a time to dance,*
> *a time to scatter stones and a time to gather them,*
> *a time to embrace and a time to*
> *refrain from embracing,*
> *a time to search and a time to give up,*
> *a time to keep and a time to throw away,*
> *a time to tear and a time to mend,*
> *a time to be silent and a time to speak,*
> *a time to love and a time to hate,*
> *a time for war and a time for peace.*

Among the many things we do with our time, we should have "a time to embrace" and "a time to love," both of which are priorities in the marriage bed.

Yet time can be elusive. It's hard to find time to do all the things you want to accomplish. Including the opportunities to nurture and savor sexual intimacy with your spouse.

Even more frustrating perhaps is that we're different in

how long it takes to "get there." So while one spouse may desire a 45-minute lovemaking session, the other could be sated with 10 minutes. Which means we have to consider what our spouse needs, negotiate with the time we have in mind, and look for ways to experience physical connection through various lengths of sexual contact—sometimes a quickie, sometimes a mid-length session, sometimes a marathon lovemaking event.

Touch and Pray

Dear Father, we don't have unlimited time for lovemaking, but we want our encounters to be satisfying and meaningful. Help us to find the time we need and want to engage in sexual intimacy. Show us where we can adjust our schedules to make time for one another and our marriage bed.

[Pray for the specifics you mentioned in your conversation.]

In the name of Your Son, Amen.

Do and Do

1. Time your next several sexual encounters. Yes, it can feel awkward to start the timer when you show up for lovemaking, then click it off when you're finished. But oftentimes, we don't have a good idea of how long we're spending, and one spouse may underestimate or overestimate how long sex takes. Having actual data could be enlightening and helpful as you discuss how long your lovemaking should last.

2. If you're prone to longer lovemaking, schedule a quickie for the coming week, making sure you have all the stuff you need ready to get going.[4] If you're given to mid-length sessions or quickies, schedule a marathon event sometime in the next month. (You get longer to accomplish this second goal, because a marathon event could harder to set up.) Either way, talk to each other afterward about the experience.

4You can find tips for having a great quickie in my book, Hot, Holy, and Humorous: Sex in Marriage by God's Design.

Chapter 14
PUCKER UP

Do you remember your first kiss? Maybe it was awkward, maybe it was amazing, but regardless, there was something special about pressing your lips together. And then came the more passionate kisses. We relished those moments of affection. But after we've been married for a while, the amount of kissing we do often falls off. Why is that? Why do we neglect one of the activities that most aroused us when we were dating, engaged, or first married?

Ask and Listen

1. Do you think we kiss enough? Why or why not?

2. What kinds of kisses do you most enjoy? Pecks, soft kisses, French kisses, or something else?

3. What could I do to kiss you better?

Read and Consider

Read together Song of Songs 1:2.

Let him kiss me with the kisses of his mouth—
for your love is more delightful than wine.

This is how the book in the Bible about sexual intimacy begins—with the woman's longing to be kissed by her beloved. To her, that very kiss demonstrates his love.

Kissing has been shown to have many benefits, including improved dental health, stress management, and the release of body chemicals that create euphoria. Women also experience an increase in testosterone, which boosts sexual desire, and men have a release of oxytocin, which creates a sense of bonding. Moreover, deep kissing is also one of three activities research has linked to women achieving orgasm.[5] With all these benefits, why aren't we doing it more often and more intensely?

Consider the last line of a typical Western-culture wedding: "And now you may kiss the bride." Perhaps we should add to the end of that sentence: "now and for the rest of your marriage."

---

[5]Davis, Nicola, and Mona Chalabi. "'Golden Trio' of Moves Boosts Chances of Female Orgasm, Say Researchers." The Guardian. February 23, 2017. Accessed September 24, 2018. https://www.theguardian.com/lifeandstyle/2017/feb/23/golden-trio-of-moves-boosts-chances-of-female-orgasm-say-researchers.

Touch and Pray

God, Your Word says several times that believers are to greet one another with a holy kiss. In marriage, our affection goes even deeper, with romantic and passionate kisses. We thank You for making our mouths capable of such closeness. Remind us to use this gift regularly to strengthen our intimacy.

[Pray for any improvements you discussed implementing.] In Jesus' name, Amen.

Do and Do

1. Set a timer for one minute and kiss for at least that long. Each day, increase your kissing time by one minute until you have kissed a full ten minutes. Compare notes about how the experience made you feel.

2. Get an ice cube and place it in one spouse's mouth, then kiss to pass it to the other. Kiss again to return the ice cube. And back and forth, back and forth, until the ice cube is melted. Variation: use ice cream, chocolate, or another melt-able food.

Pillow Talk

Chapter 15

CONFESSION IS GOOD
FOR THE SOUL

It's an old Scottish proverb: "Open confession is good for the soul." While we nod and agree that it's good for the soul, we also fear—often rightly—that confession is hard on relationships. Admitting past or current secrets to your spouse is likely to result in hurt and even anger. But without vulnerability and authenticity, we can never reach intimacy and healing.

Ask and Listen

1. What was the hardest thing you've ever told me about your sexuality or our sexual intimacy?

2. What response would you like me to have when you confess something difficult?[6]

3. What, if any, struggles are you facing that I don't fully know about and that could impact our sexual intimacy?

---

[6]You are not obligated to react the way your spouse desires. But their response to this question can illuminate what fears they have in confessing to you.

Read and Consider

Read together Proverbs 28:13 and Numbers 5:6-7.

Whoever conceals their sins does not prosper, but the one who confesses and renounces them finds mercy.

Say to the Israelites: "Any man or woman who wrongs another in any way and so is unfaithful to the Lord is guilty and must confess the sin they have committed. They must make full restitution for the wrong they have done, add a fifth of the value to it and give it all to the person they have wronged."

We dread confessing our sins, especially to the one we've wronged. And yet, the Bible says we will not prosper and we are unfaithful to the Lord until we have confessed and renounced our sins. Following confession, we should, in any way we can, heal the relationship—making "restitution," which is simply restoring to someone what they deserve.

Since our spouse deserves our sexual interest, focus, and intimacy, we need to confess anything that has impaired our one-flesh covenant. We will receive mercy from God and then we can plan out the path to healing for our marriage. Yes, confession can be a challenge for marriage, but secret sins are far more costly.

Touch and Pray

Lord, we confess our sins and our struggles, knowing that You will forgive us. We call upon You as our refuge and our strength as we face our individual struggles as one-flesh in our marriage. Help us to be honest, supportive, and loving of one another.

[Pray about the confessions you made in your conversation.]

In Jesus' name, Amen.

Do and Do

1. Write a letter to your spouse expressing your feelings about whatever he or she confessed during your conversation. Be honest and open about your hurt, your anger, and your fears. Let your heart flow onto the page. When finished, pray about your feelings and then take the letter and either tear it up or tuck it away. (If you decide you need marital counseling, this letter could be useful later, but consult your counselor before sharing.)

2. For anything you confessed, find a quiet place and time on your own and pray the following prayer from David (Psalm 51:1-10):

Have mercy on me, O God,
because of your unfailing love.
Because of your great compassion,
blot out the stain of my sins.
Wash me clean from my guilt
Purify me from my sin.
For I recognize my rebellion;
it haunts me day and night.
Against you, and you alone, have I sinned;
I have done what is evil in your sight.
You will be proved right in what you say,
and your judgment against me is just.
For I was born a sinner—
yes, from the moment my mother conceived me.
But you desire honesty from the womb,
teaching me wisdom even there.
Purify me from my sins, and I will be clean;
wash me, and I will be whiter than snow.
Oh, give me back my joy again;
you have broken me—
now let me rejoice.
Don't keep looking at my sins.
Remove the stain of my guilt.
Create in me a clean heart, O God.
Renew a loyal spirit within me.

Chapter 16
HAS PORN AFFECTED US?

Our culture is inundated with pornography, with increased availability and societal acceptance driving much of the increase in porn viewing and habits. However, we now have ample evidence of its negative effect on individuals and on marriage.

Ask and Listen

1. When and how was your first exposure to porn? What do you remember feeling when you saw it?

2. Do you believe you've had a problem with porn? Why or why not?

3. Be honest: Are you currently struggling with porn? If so, how can I help?

Read and Consider

Read together 1 Thessalonians 4:3-7.

It is God's will that you should be sanctified: that you should avoid sexual immorality; that each of you should learn to control your own body in a way that is holy and honorable, not in passionate lust like the pagans, who do not know God; and that in this matter no one should wrong or take advantage of a brother or sister. The Lord will punish all those who commit such sins, as we told you and warned you before. For God did not call us to be impure, but to live a holy life.

Pornography stokes "passionate lust" that takes advantage of others. But it's so prevalent in our culture that it's difficult to avoid seeing it at one time or another. No longer does one have to seek out the nudie magazine to view pornography—it's available with a few clicks or even pops up on websites when we don't expect it. And sexual imagery that should count as pornographic appears on TV series and movies that stop short of an X-rating.

Unfortunately, all this exposure means that one's view of sexuality can be tainted by porn. We receive erroneous messages about what sex should look like, about which practices are appealing and pleasurable, about pursuing selfish satisfaction in the bedroom. Porn encourages us to treat our lover as a tool for our sexual pleasure, rather than a partner in mutual sexual intimacy.

God calls us away from impurity to a holy life, including holiness in the marriage bed with sex as God intended—exclusive, mutual, pleasurable, and even spiritual.

Touch and Pray

*Dear Father, we pour out our hearts to You,
sharing our temptations and our struggles and
asking for Your guidance and strength in pursuing
the right path. Direct our thoughts, our feelings,
and our choices. Help us to see others not as tools
for our pleasure, but rather as Your children
who deserve respect. Give us unity in support-
ing one another's walk of sexual purity, helping
us to focus entirely on our own marriage bed.*

*[Pray for the challenges you brought
up during your discussion.]*

*And Father, we pray that You will marshal your
forces to fight against the prevalence of porn in our
society, the sexual trafficking that goes along with
it, and the destruction it causes to individuals
and marriages. Help us to be part of that battle.*

In Jesus' name, Amen.

Do and Do

1. If porn has been a problem with either one of you, look into filtering software that can keep pornography from being easily accessed on your computer and mobile devices. Covenant Eyes is one potential source.

2. If either of you has struggled with porn, reach out for help. XXX Church and Dirty Girls Ministries provide resources for Christians wanting to break free from persistent porn use and the damaging views left in its wake.

Chapter 17
REBUILDING TRUST IN THE BEDROOM

To give yourself intimately to your spouse, you must lower your defenses, get naked, allow someone to touch and kiss the most private parts of your body, and join physically to another. There is an emotional and spiritual unveiling of yourself in all of this too. Trust is, therefore, a key component for the marriage bed. Conflict and betrayal in the course of our marriage can break our trust. How can we rebuild it?

Ask and Listen

1. What past or present experiences in our marriage have made it difficult for you to trust me fully?

2. How has a lack of complete trust affected our sexual intimacy?

3. What would you be more open to if I could prove my trustworthiness to you?

Read and Consider

Read together 1 Corinthians 4:2.

Now it is required that those who have
been given a trust must prove faithful.

The Bible doesn't command us to trust others without reason. Rather, like the verse above, the Word of God focuses on being trustworthy (see also Proverbs 12:22, Luke 16:10, and 1 Timothy 3:11). Thus, it's reasonable to discern whether someone is worthy of our trust.

Our spouse needs to believe overall that we have their best interests at heart. When betrayal—intentional or unintentional—has occurred, repentance and forgiveness are one step, but restoring trust is another. And it can take time.

Negotiate what each of you needs to trust, and make every effort to provide your spouse their request. It may seem over-the-top to you—for instance, reporting regularly on your whereabouts—but why not go overboard to show your beloved that you can be trusted? Make it clear to your spouse that you are all-in on providing a safe place for sexual intimacy to happen and thrive.

Touch and Pray

We place our trust in You, Lord, and in Your ways. You created the marriage bed to be a place of vulnerability and intimacy, and we pray that we will pursue one another's trust and provide a sense of safety in our sex life. Help us to rebuild the trust that we have lost, remembering that we will let each other down at times but that we can rely on our commitment and love.

[Pray for the steps you need to take in your marriage to rebuild trust.]

In the name of Jesus Christ, Amen.

Go and Do

1. List what words your spouse could say or actions they could take that would help you trust them more. Make sure your list isn't about keeping a record of wrongs (see 1 Corinthians 13:5), but genuine steps you need for your trust to be rebuilt. Then share your list with your spouse.

2. List three steps you will take to demonstrate to your spouse that you are worthy of their trust, especially when it comes to sexual intimacy. Post the list somewhere so that you will be reminded regularly to follow through. Then follow through.

Pillow Talk

Chapter 18
WHAT ABOUT SEX TOYS?

A common question about physical intimacy in marriage is whether it can or should include marital aids or "sex toys." Inclusion of these props in the marriage bed has increased in recent years, especially with the anonymity of online purchasing and offerings even from Christian-based stores. Since the Bible does not explicitly approve or disapprove of this practice, the question of whether to use sex toys relies on Christian principles, practical concerns, and personal preference.

Ask and Listen

1. What is your general feeling about marital aids or sex toys?

2. In what ways could such aids assist our lovemaking? In what ways could they detract from it?

3. Are there any aids in particular you'd like to try and, if so, why?

Read and Consider

Read together 1 Corinthians 10:23-24.

"I have the right to do anything," you say—but not everything is beneficial. "I have the right to do anything"—but not everything is constructive. No one should seek their own good, but the good of others.

This passage is similar to one in 1 Corinthians 6, a chapter that addresses sexual immorality, so applying this principle in the context of physical intimacy is sound. That is, having a right to do something does not mean it's a good idea. Although we'd like clear guidelines for every particular situation, some practices are not right nor wrong so much as wise or unwise, depending on circumstances and the people involved.

For example, one couple may use a marital aid to alleviate a problem like vaginal dryness, loss of erection, or extreme difficulty with orgasm—in the same way we wear glasses to correct vision. And this adds to their sexual intimacy. Another couple may use a sex toy to bypass learning how to arouse one another with just their bodies. And this detracts from their sexual intimacy.

Although some toys are not advisable under any circumstances—such as those that cause harm to your partner—many are neither good nor bad. The intent and usage determine whether they can and should be included in your marriage bed. Without a direct command from God, you must decide privately and together what reflects the intimacy you want to have.

Touch and Pray

*Dear God, in all things we want to honor You,
including the pleasure we seek in our marriage
bed. Give us wisdom to determine if and how
we will use marital aids or sex toys in our sexual
intimacy. Help us to respect one another's viewpoint
and gain unity in our choices—always applying
the principle that whatever we include should
be beneficial and constructive for both of us.*

*[Pray for what you specifically need
to make decisions together.]*

In Jesus' name, Amen.

Go and Do

1. Together, visit a Christian-based online store that sells items such as personal lubricant and marital aids. Talk about what does or doesn't appeal to you and decide whether to purchase an item to try. Make sure the decision is mutual.

You will not be exposed to any sexually graphic images using these recommended sites:

Marriage Spice

Honoring Intimates

Covenant Spice

2. Create your own marital aid. An addition to your marriage bed doesn't need to require batteries or send you off to the moon. Simple objects can assist in getting you aroused without taking away the opportunity to be hands-on with one another. Try one of the following in your next lovemaking session: rub a melting ice cube over your spouse's skin, use a feather to stroke your spouse's skin and private areas, tie a necktie or bandanna around your spouse's eyes to enhance the other four senses, give each other massages with lotion or oil, put chocolate syrup or whipping cream on your spouse's body and lick it off (being careful not to get anything into openings).

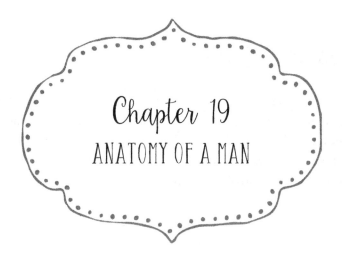

Chapter 19
ANATOMY OF A MAN

How much do you really know about the male body? If you're the husband, you might have answered, "A lot." Even the wife may believe she knows her husband's body inside and out, having seen, touched, and made love with it plenty of times. But learning the specifics of how God created the male body can help each of you know how to make the most of what he has—exploring, stimulating, and satisfying you even more.

Ask and Listen

1.   Separately study the illustration shown below and fill in as many blanks as possible, naming the parts of the male genitalia. Then see the answers in Appendix B and ask each other: How well did you do? What were you surprised that you answered correctly or missed?

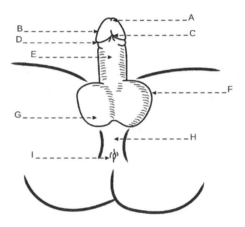

2.   *On this question, let her answer first, then him:* What do you think are the most sensitive parts on a man's body? Include within the genitalia and elsewhere on his body.

3.   *Him to her:* Where do you most like to touch my body? What arouses you? *Her to him:* Where do you most like me to touch your body? What arouses you?

Read and Consider

Read together Song of Songs 5:10-16.

My beloved is radiant and ruddy,
outstanding among ten thousand.
His head is purest gold;
his hair is wavy
and black as a raven.
His eyes are like doves
by the water streams,
washed in milk,
mounted like jewels.
His cheeks are like beds of spice
yielding perfume.
His lips are like lilies
dripping with myrrh.
His arms are rods of gold
set with topaz.
His body is like polished ivory
decorated with lapis lazuli.
His legs are pillars of marble
set on bases of pure gold.
His appearance is like Lebanon,
choice as its cedars.
His mouth is sweetness itself;
he is altogether lovely.
This is my beloved, this is my friend,
daughters of Jerusalem.

The imagery this wife uses is fascinating. She begins with tender word pictures—comparing his eyes to doves, his lips to lilies—but when she gets below his neck, she is immediately aware of his strength and solidness—comparing his arms to rods of gold, his body to ivory, his legs to marble.

Indeed, the male body is different from a female's in so many ways. Not only are our external genitalia different, but men are typically larger; exhibit greater upper body strength; have greater endurance; have stronger bones, tendons, and ligaments; have larger hearts, thicker skin, and more body hair; and, of course, make more testosterone.

As a result, husbands may desire different types of touches with more pressure or friction. For instance, more than one husband has reported that her digging a fingernail into his shoulder or biting his arm or chest isn't painful but pleasurable. What matters, however, is your own husband's body and what he enjoys. It's ultimately not about the anatomy of *a* man, but the anatomy of the man in your marriage bed.

Touch and Pray

Dear Lord, thank You so much for creating us male and female, with distinct differences and appeal. Help us to fully appreciate the male body as You provisioned it. We pray Your blessing on us as we both explore this body in our marriage bed and find ways to experience greater pleasure and intimacy.

[Pray about any concerns brought up in your discussion.]

In the name of Jesus and through the Holy Spirit, Amen.

Go and Do

1. Using the above Bible passage as an example, have the wife make a list of the parts of his body that most appeal to her and why. You can use comparisons or explanations or poetry, but express what you appreciate about how God made his body. Then have the wife share what she wrote with her husband.

2. Have him get naked, and have her stay clothed (though she can wear something provocative). Starting at the top of his head, have the wife move her hand slowly, slowly, slowly down his body. As she touches him, the husband should report what feels good and how she can adjust the pressure of her strokes to his liking. Make sure to end this exercise with her touching his genitals.

Pillow Talk

Chapter 20
ANATOMY OF A WOMAN

However complex the male body is, the woman's body seems even more so—particularly because his genitalia have been out there for him to see and touch since birth, while her genitalia are more hidden, like a treasure to be discovered. In addition, women's bodies change substantially over time, so that her body while pregnant or after childbirth can feel quite different from before, including such seemingly small things as how she experiences temperature or her sense of smell. Knowing how God created a woman's body, and how this particular wife's body is made, can help you make sexual intimacy an enjoyable experience for both of you.

Ask and Listen

1. Separately study the illustration shown below and fill in as many blanks as possible, naming the parts of the female genitalia. Then see the answers in Appendix C ask each other: How well did you do? What were you surprised that you answered correctly or missed?

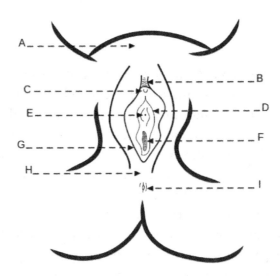

2. *On this question, let him answer first, then her:* What do you think are the most sensitive parts on a woman's body? Include within the genitalia and elsewhere on her body.

3. *Her to him:* Where do you most like to touch my body? What arouses you? *Him to her:* Where do you most like me to touch your body? What arouses you?

Read and Consider

Read together Song of Songs 7:1-6.

How beautiful your sandaled feet,
  O prince's daughter!
Your graceful legs are like jewels,
  the work of an artist's hands.
Your navel is a rounded goblet
  that never lacks blended wine.
Your waist is a mound of wheat
  encircled by lilies.
Your breasts are like two fawns,
  like twin fawns of a gazelle.
Your neck is like an ivory tower.
Your eyes are the pools of Heshbon
  by the gate of Bath Rabbim.
Your nose is like the tower of Lebanon
  looking toward Damascus.
Your head crowns you like Mount Carmel.
  Your hair is like royal tapestry;
  the king is held captive by its tresses.
How beautiful you are and how pleasing,
  my love, with your delights!

Remember reading the wife's breakdown of her husband's body in the last chapter? This time, it's the husband describing his wife, and the imagery is flipped. When it comes to her body, the husband uses gentle pictures—calling her legs graceful, her navel rounded, her breasts fawns. But above the shoulders, he gives firmer language to what he sees—her neck and nose like towers, her head like Mount Carmel. Instinctively, he understands the differences between male and female bodies.

Women have a larger and broader pelvis and a higher percentage of body fat, which makes for those rounded curves. They have smoother and generally lighter skin. Their sense of smell is better, and they have more language processing areas in their brains. Women have a faster heartbeat, lower blood pressure overall, and more pain receptors.

These differences make women sensitive in different ways, including the kind of touches they prefer—typically softer and slower, at least at first. Take time and effort to appreciate what makes a woman's body beautiful and special, particularly the wife in your marriage.

Touch and Pray

Dear Lord, when man needed a helper, You created woman and made her suitable but different in wonderful ways. We thank You for the function and beauty of a woman's body. Be with us as we explore and experience the pleasure and intimacy of the female body in our marriage bed.

[Pray for any concerns brought up in your discussion.]

In Jesus and through the Spirit we pray, Amen.

Go and Do

1. It's his turn. Using the above Bible passage as an example, have the husband make a list of the parts of her body that most appeal to him and why. You can use comparisons or explanations or poetry, but express what you appreciate about how God made her body. Then have the husband share what he wrote with his wife.

2. Have her get naked, and have him stay clothed (though he can wear something enticing). Starting at the top of her head, have the husband move his hand slowly, slowly, slowly down her body. As he touches her, the wife should report what feels good and how he can adjust the pressure of his caresses to her liking. Make sure to end this exercise with touching her genitalia.

Pillow Talk

Chapter 21
COMMUNICATING DURING SEX

It can be awkward enough to talk about sex with your mate at first, but even more so *during* sex. We may struggle to express our thoughts and feelings and feel self-conscious about the sounds we make. Yet it can also be very arousing and reassuring to your mate to not only see but also hear your pleasure, and we should be able to communicate what we desire in the marriage bed.

Ask and Listen

1. Have you ever wanted something during sexual intimacy but felt awkward asking for it? Why?

2. What sounds or words would you like to hear me make during lovemaking? What would arouse and/or reassure you?

3. Have I used words or sounds that are a turn-off to you? If so, which ones and why?

Read and Consider

Read together Song of Songs 2:8-10.

> *Listen! My beloved!*
> *Look! Here he comes,*
> *leaping across the mountains,*
> *bounding over the hills.*
> *My beloved is like a gazelle or a young stag.*
> *Look! There he stands behind our wall,*
> *gazing through the windows,*
> *peering through the lattice.*
> *My beloved spoke and said to me,*
> *"Arise, my darling,*
> *my beautiful one, come with me."*

This wife remembers not only seeing her beloved husband approach, but what he *said* to her. His tender words lingered in her mind as a sweet memory of their intimacy.

Likewise, we remember words spoken to us, especially when they are used to build us up in meaningful ways. During sexual intimacy, we have an opportunity to express deep love for one another, using speech and sounds that show our engagement, excitement, and ecstasy.

Are you using that opportunity? Perhaps you can use it better by allowing yourself to express what you think, want, and feel in the moment.

Touch and Pray

Lord, Your Word often addresses how we can use our speech either to tear down or to build up others. We long to build one another up in our marriage and in our sexual intimacy. Help us feel free to express positive words and desires that increase our arousal and satisfaction in the marriage bed.

[Pray about your challenges in communicating during sex.]

We praise You and pray in the Spirit and the name of Jesus Christ, Amen.

Go and Do

1. Look back at what your spouse said they'd like to hear in bed. The next time you make love, try to meet one of their requests. Even if it feels weird the first time, you might discover it's arousing and appreciated.

2. It can be particularly stimulating to hear your name spoken during lovemaking. In your next encounter, use your spouse's name at least once during foreplay, once during intercourse, and once during orgasm. Share afterward how it felt to hear your beloved say your name during sexual intimacy.

Pillow Talk

Chapter 22
ARE WE COMPARING?

William Shakespeare wrote, "Shall I compare thee to a summer's day? Thou art more lovely and more temperate.[7]" But many spouses don't feel they're compared to summer days or other metaphors, but rather previous sexual partners, porn actors, romance fiction heroes, or even the latest cover model on a magazine at the grocery store checkout. And as lovely and temperate as we may be, we worry about whether we measure up.

Ask and Listen

1. Are you concerned that I compare you or your body to other people? If so, in what way?

2. Have you struggled with comparing me to other people? If so, how?

3. What would help you believe that my current desire is only for you?

[7]Shakespeare, William. "Sonnet 18: Shall I Compare Thee to a Summer's Day? by William Shakespeare." Poetry Foundation. Accessed March 27, 2018. https://www.poetryfoundation.org/poems/45087/sonnet-18-shall-i-compare-thee-to-a-summers-day.

Read and Consider

Read together Song of Songs 5:9-10 and 6:8-9 (NLT).

> Friends: *How is your beloved better than others,*
> *most beautiful of women?*
> *How is your beloved better than others,*
> *that you so charge us?*

> She: *My beloved is radiant and ruddy,*
> *outstanding among ten thousand.*

> He: *Even among sixty queens*
> *and eighty concubines*
> *and countless young women,*
> *I would still choose my dove, my perfect one—*
> *the favorite of her mother,*
> *dearly loved by the one who bore her.*

These lovers in Song of Songs compare their mates to others—but only long enough to say that he outshines the rest and she is the perfect one he would choose among many. Spouses should feel safe that they are loved and accepted for who they are, above all others.

This doesn't mean we're ignorant of the attractiveness of others or the sexual past we may have had, but rather we choose to show daily that our spouse is the only one we want to be sexual with.

If your spouse doesn't know that he is "outstanding among ten thousand" or she is "my perfect one," it's time to express that sentiment more clearly. Conversely, when your spouse says that you are outstanding or perfect, believe them. The vast majority of the time, spouses are not comparing you to other options or lovers—they chose you and want to be with you.

Touch and Pray

*God, Your Word says that You are a jealous God;
as our bridegroom, You long for our faithfulness.
Likewise, in our marriage, we long to have one
another's sole romantic attention, to be seen and
cherished for who we are. Help us to keep our eyes
and thoughts on one another, to avoid the temptation of others, and to express our commitment
and desire for one another without question.*

[Pray for struggles and goals you discussed earlier.]

In Jesus' name, Amen.

Go and Do

1. If you have compared your spouse to others, get rid of
any reminders of that temptation. Kick porn to the curb,
starting with internet filtering software. Toss out the romance
novels that make you ruminate about the latest fictional hero.
Purge the photo album of old girlfriend or boyfriend photos
you really don't need. "Unfriend" your ex on social media.
Remember that your marriage should take priority, so demonstrate commitment to your spouse through action.

2. Write a letter or poem to your spouse expressing how you feel about him or her. Be sure to tell your beloved that you don't desire anyone else and that you want all of your sexual intimacy to be focused on the one you married. Trade letters.[8]

---

[8]Tips for writing a well-received love letter are in my book, *Hot, Holy, and Humorous: Sex and Marriage by God's Design.*

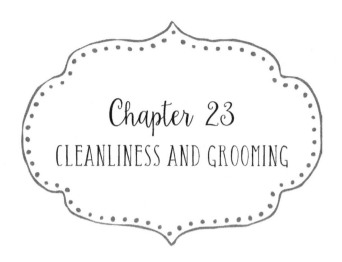

Chapter 23
CLEANLINESS AND GROOMING

Imagine a *Family Feud* game show question: "We polled one hundred wives and asked, 'What's one reason you sometimes don't want to be intimate with your husband?'" Lack of hygiene and grooming would likely make the board. But it isn't only wives but also husbands who desire their spouse to be clean and well-groomed. We are turned off by unhygienic bodies, unkempt appearance, and offensive smells. It's prudent and pleasing to keep yourself cleaned and groomed, especially for the intimate contact of lovemaking.

Ask and Listen

1. How often do you think we should shower? Wash our hair?

2. What kind of cleaning or grooming would you like me to do before we make love?

3. Do you like me wearing cologne or perfume or some other product? What would smell good to you?

Read and Consider

Read together Song of Songs 1:3 and 4:9-10.

She: *Pleasing is the fragrance of your perfumes; your name is like perfume poured out. No wonder the young women love you!*

He: *You have stolen my heart, my sister, my bride;*
you have stolen my heart
with one glance of your eyes,
with one jewel of your necklace.
How delightful is your love, my sister, my bride!
How much more pleasing is your love than wine,
and the fragrance of your perfume
more than any spice!

Smell is a particularly important sense when it comes to cleanliness and grooming. Women tend to have a better sense of smell and thus may be more sensitive to his scent. But both husband and wife in the Song of Songs comment on one another's "perfume"—naming it as one of the appeals of their lover.

Likewise, we should pay attention to our hygiene and present ourselves well to our lover. Let your spouse have some say about your cleanliness and grooming, since you are inviting them to enjoy your body too.

Touch and Pray

*Dear Lord, thank You for giving us our senses of
sight, touch, smell, and taste—all of which can
detect cleanliness and grooming. Help us to be
respectable of our spouse's senses and to present our
bodies for lovemaking in ways that are appealing.*

[Pray about any issues you need to address.]

We pray in Jesus' name, Amen.

Do and Do

1. Take a bath or shower together, and wash one another. Let the spouse washing take charge of making sure every area of their beloved's body is as clean as they wish. Each of you should take note of what your spouse did so that you can later clean to the same level yourself.

2. Take a trip to a perfumery or the department or grocery store sample counter. Try out various samples on one another and talk about what you like and don't like. If financially feasible, find a mutually agreeable scent for each of you and purchase it to try at home.

Pillow Talk

Chapter 24
WHAT ABOUT BODY HAIR?

In ancient Egypt, both men and women of the higher classes removed all body hair, excluding their eyebrows. In contrast, full body hair was acceptable in most cultures a hundred years ago. In today's Western culture, most women are expected to shave their armpits, legs, and at least trim their pubic area. Meanwhile, men's facial hair varies from clean-shaved to trimmed mustaches to every kind of beard imaginable, including a full lion's mane, and many men manage the hair on their bodies. But what about our preferences for the marriage bed?

Ask and Listen

1. How often do you like to shave, wax, or trim (yourself) and where?

2. Where would you like me to do more body hair trimming or removal? Why?

3. Would you be willing to trim or remove as I suggested and see how it affects our lovemaking? Why or why not?

Read and Consider

Read together Genesis 2:25.

Adam and his wife were both naked,
and they felt no shame.

There's no specific scripture about body or pubic hair, and when the lovers of Song of Songs comment on one another's hair, let's hope their description wasn't about the pubic area ("Your hair is like a flock of goats descending from the hills of Gilead" (4:1); "his hair is wavy and black as a raven" (5:11)). No, thanks.

But being naked before one another was certainly in God's plan. And nakedness can involve as much skin or hair as we have and want to display. Some people are hairier, and some are smoother, but how much hair they have can affect accessibility and sensations experienced during sexual pleasure.[9]

When Joseph was summoned to come before Pharaoh, he washed himself and shaved, likely removing all body hair in line with current custom. So we know at least one God-fearing man in the Bible was shaved and naked with his wife. Without command to the contrary, and at least one example of shaving in this way, it seems that body hair trimming or removal is a choice for individuals and couples to make.

---

[9]Some wives express concern that their husband's desire for less pubic hair on her might be related to porn use or a desire for a girlish appearance. However, husbands often say it's about seeing her genitalia more clearly, having improved access to her vulva, and experiencing different sensations during lovemaking.

Touch and Pray

Lord, You created our bodies with skin hair of varying amounts. We know that various people in the Bible cut the hair on their heads, so grooming has long been acceptable among Your people. Please help us to accept one another's bodies and beauty while also making decisions about how we will cut or trim our body hair to provide the pleasure in appearance and sensation during lovemaking that we desire.

[Pray for any specifics, particularly any fear you may have over this issue.]

In the name of Your Son Jesus, Amen.

Do and Do

1. Allow your spouse to trim or shave you. Don't panic. Gather all the products necessary and coach your spouse on how to shave you. Use an electric trimmer at a mid-setting or a razor specifically made for the bikini area that won't shave too close. If your skin is sensitive, apply an aftershave product to keep your skin smooth and healthy. (Be careful to avoid the aftershave getting into any openings down there!)

2. Surprise your spouse by trimming, shaving, or waxing in the way you discussed above. You might consider adding a temporary tattoo or sticky-jewels to highlight the area. After making love, discuss if and how the sensations were different.

Pillow Talk

Chapter 25
DO YOU NEED MORE FOREPLAY?

We tend to believe that wives require more foreplay than husbands, and that's mostly true. However, some lower-desire husbands and aging men also need more foreplay to reach readiness for sexual intercourse. Regardless, most couples don't spend enough time in foreplay to prepare their bodies for sexual intimacy, and to simply enjoy the many pleasures of the marriage bed.

Ask and Listen

1. What do you define as foreplay? What actions arouse you toward readiness for lovemaking?

2. Do you believe we spend enough time in foreplay? Why or why not?

3. What touches, kisses, or activities would you like us to focus on more in foreplay?

Read and Consider

Read together Song of Songs 2:3-6.

Like an apple tree among the trees of the forest
is my beloved among the young men.
I delight to sit in his shade,
and his fruit is sweet to my taste.
Let him lead me to the banquet hall,
and let his banner over me be love.
Strengthen me with raisins,
refresh me with apples,
for I am faint with love.
His left arm is under my head,
and his right arm embraces me.

While we cannot say for sure, many biblical scholars believe that "his fruit is sweet to my taste" and "his right arm embraces me" refer to oral sex and fondling respectively. Regardless, in eight chapters of a book on marital, sexual love, only a few verses refer specifically to intercourse. The rest of the time, this biblical couple is engaged in describing and delighting one another's bodies. That is to say, they are enjoying foreplay.

Of course, what foreplay looks like for one couple may be different from what appeals to another, but physical intimacy should involve the whole person, not just the sex bits. Attending to your beloved's full body will be more arousing for both of you and more satisfying when you reach intercourse.

Touch and Pray

God, we thank You for creating our bodies to feel pleasure. Help us to attend to one another's full bodies and to enjoy the many activities and experiences that make up our sexual arousal and satisfaction.

[Pray about the foreplay goals you discussed.]

In Jesus' name, Amen.

Do and Do

1. Take off your shoes and any jewelry you usually remove, but leave your clothes on. Keeping yourselves clothed, see how much foreplay you can engage in. You may use your hand or mouth to shift clothing or reach underneath, but don't unbutton or unzip. Spend at least fifteen minutes exploring how much you can arouse each other *with your clothes on* before getting naked and enjoying your bare bodies together.

2. Get a timer and set it for ten minutes. Have one spouse spend those ten full minutes providing foreplay for their mate, attending to what you discussed and agreed upon. When the ten minutes are up, reset the timer and switch so that the receiver becomes the giver. When the full twenty minutes are up, use the time however you wish. Variation: Increase the time to fifteen minutes, twenty, or more. (Note that some spouses can take forty-five minutes or more to reach climax.)

Pillow Talk

Chapter 26
FAMILY PLANNING

God values families. And families can be large, medium, small, or simply two people—husband and wife. Getting on the same page with sexual intimacy involves making decisions about the size of your family, your timing, and your approach toward conception and contraception.

Ask and Listen

1. What principles should guide our decisions about family planning and birth control?

2. What would you like us to change about our approach to family planning?[10]

3. What kind of contraception, if any, would you like for us to consider and why?

---

[10]This can include "I want more kids" or "I'm ready to have kids" or "I want to be done." Tailor your answer to whichever season you're in.

Read and Consider

Read together 1 Samuel 1:1-20.

*There was a certain man from Ramathaim,
a Zuphite from the hill country of Ephraim,
whose name was Elkanah son of Jeroham,
the son of Elihu, the son of Tohu, the son of
Zuph, an Ephraimite. He had two wives; one
was called Hannah and the other Peninnah.
Peninnah had children, but Hannah had none.*

*Year after year this man went up from his town
to worship and sacrifice to the Lord Almighty at
Shiloh, where Hophni and Phinehas, the two
sons of Eli, were priests of the Lord. Whenever the
day came for Elkanah to sacrifice, he would give
portions of the meat to his wife Peninnah and
to all her sons and daughters. But to Hannah he
gave a double portion because he loved her, and
the Lord had closed her womb. Because the Lord
had closed Hannah's womb, her rival kept provok-
ing her in order to irritate her. This went on year
after year. Whenever Hannah went up to the
house of the Lord, her rival provoked her till she
wept and would not eat. Her husband Elkanah
would say to her, "Hannah, why are you weeping?
Why don't you eat? Why are you downhearted?
Don't I mean more to you than ten sons?"*

*Once when they had finished eating and drinking
in Shiloh, Hannah stood up. Now Eli the priest*

was sitting on his chair by the doorpost of the Lord's house. In her deep anguish Hannah prayed to the Lord, weeping bitterly. And she made a vow, saying, "Lord Almighty, if you will only look on your servant's misery and remember me, and not forget your servant but give her a son, then I will give him to the Lord for all the days of his life, and no razor will ever be used on his head."

As she kept on praying to the Lord, Eli observed her mouth. Hannah was praying in her heart, and her lips were moving but her voice was not heard. Eli thought she was drunk and said to her, "How long are you going to stay drunk? Put away your wine."

"Not so, my lord," Hannah replied, "I am a woman who is deeply troubled. I have not been drinking wine or beer; I was pouring out my soul to the Lord. Do not take your servant for a wicked woman; I have been praying here out of my great anguish and grief."

Eli answered, "Go in peace, and may the God of Israel grant you what you have asked of him."

She said, "May your servant find favor in your eyes." Then she went her way and ate something, and her face was no longer downcast.

Early the next morning they arose and worshiped before the Lord and then went back to their home at Ramah. Elkanah made love to his wife Hannah, and the Lord remembered her. So in the course of time Hannah became pregnant and gave birth to a son. She named him Samuel, saying, "Because I asked the Lord for him."

We don't have specific passages in the Bible that address contraception. But we can discern some takeaways from stories like Hannah's.

1. Children are considered a blessing. Hannah longed to have children, and her desire is seen as good while her grief is seen as reasonable.

2. Not having children doesn't diminish the validity of your marriage. Hannah's husband Elkanah loved her no less and reassured her that their bond meant more to him than having children ("ten sons").

3. There is a time for everything, including pregnancy. Even after Eli blesses Hannah, the passage says "in the course of time Hannah became pregnant." Likewise, we may need to consider the right course of time for the arrival of children into our home.

Touch and Pray

Dear God, we know that children are a blessing to individual families, to communities, and to the world. It was through a family that Your brought Your Son into the world, though not everyone who has served You faithfully has had their own children. Help us to understand our role in having children, and give us unity in making our decisions. Bless us with the children You want us to have, and help us to understand and honor Your will throughout.

[Pray about issues brought up in your discussion time.]

In the name of Your Son, Amen.

Go and Do

1. If you made a decision to research or try a different contraceptive method, follow through. Make an appointment with the doctor, research birth control alternatives, purchase what you need, etc.

2. If you're not on the same page about how many kids you desire or the timing of children, make a promise to think through one another's answer and schedule an appointment on your calendar to discuss this topic again. It can be one week in the future or one month, but no more than three months. In the meantime, pray that God will give you unity in your decision.

Pillow Talk

Chapter 27
HER CYCLES

Most women recall the first time they learned about menstruation. Despite all efforts to wrap that conversation in a big smile and the phrase "you're becoming a woman," many of us were suspicious about having a period once a month. Once introduced to the products that handled that experience—mini-pads, maxi-pads, tampons, menstrual cups—we became even more sure this was not the definition of fun. Add hormones to the mix, and we concluded someone should call the spa and book us an appointment for all-day pampering. Then when we got married, our husbands got to learn a bit of what it's like to deal with a woman's cycle. Though maybe she, he, or both still don't know quite as much as they could or should.11

---

[11] If the wife is past menstruation, you might want to move on to the next chapter on Menopause.

Ask and Listen

1. *Him to her only*: What was the onset of menstruation like for you? How did you learn about it, and what were your experiences with periods when you were younger?

2. How do you think the wife's cycle affects our sex life?

3. How could we better plan our sexual intimacy with the wife's cycle in mind?

Read and Consider

Read together 1 Peter 3:7.

> *Husbands, in the same way be consider-*
> *ate as you live with your wives, and treat*
> *them with respect as the weaker partner and*
> *as heirs with you of the gracious gift of life,*
> *so that nothing will hinder your prayers.*

Changes in mood and desire for sex are often a part of a woman's natural cycle. These variations can be frustrating for both wife and husband to gauge and address. Some wives also experience intense pain and discomfort before or during their period. Periods can take sexual intercourse off the table.[12]

---

[12]Some couples continue to engage in sexual intercourse during a period, either ignoring the "mess" or using a condom or menstrual cup to minimize blood-skin contact. Old Testament laws about avoiding sex during a woman's period are typically viewed by Christian scholars as among those regulations intended for the time in which the Israelites lived and not for today's Christians, but each person and couple should live according to their conscience. While there is an increased risk of infection during a woman's period, many engage without problems. Simply do your homework and

While being called "weaker" comes across poorly to many women, Peter's statement is biologically true, in that women tend to have less physical strength and endurance, as well as challenges like menstruation. In light of that, Peter encourages husbands to be considerate and treat their wives with respect. That includes how a woman's cycle—her natural, God-given physiology—is handled in your marriage and your marriage bed.

Consider what effects the wife's cycle can or will have on your sexual intimacy and plan accordingly. Look for ways to minimize her discomfort and still pursue sexual pleasure and intimacy when and how you can. Intercourse may be off the table, but other sexual acts can be experienced and enjoyed as you desire.

Touch and Pray

Holy Father, Your design for reproduction is beautiful but marred by the broken world we live in. While a wife's cycles are a gift, the way we experience them can be challenging—both to us as individuals and to our marriage bed. Give us wisdom and unity in addressing any challenges we face.

[Pray specifically about your issues related to the wife's cycle.]

In the holy name of Jesus, Amen.

respect one another's feelings on this topic.

Do and Do

1. Use a calendar or download a tracking app, and keep track of her cycle for at least a month. Make sure the husband also has access to the information, so he knows when the wife is experiencing each stage (menstruation, follicular phase, ovulation, and luteal phase). Add notes on days when she feels more amenable toward sex and days when she is less so, then discuss how this affects your sexual intimacy.

2. Take a trip to the grocery or discount store and walk the feminine hygiene aisle together. Let her explain the various products in the aisles, what they're for, how they work, and what she prefers to use and why. For husbands, this is a good time to take notes about her choices, in case you ever need to go shopping on her behalf. Yes, you might someday, and if you do, she'll appreciate it.

Chapter 28
MENOPAUSE

Menopause means the absence of a period for twelve months. What we tend to call menopause is actually perimenopause or menopausal transition—the female body slowly changing from regular reproductive cycles to an absence of ovulation and menstruation. That phase usually takes four to five years, but can take up to ten.[13] Did you both realize this when you married? And did you fully consider how it might impact your sex life?

Ask and Listen

1. *Him to her*: Where are you in perimenopause or menopause? What symptoms have you experienced as part of your body's changes?

2. How do you believe perimenopause and/or menopause impacts our sex life?

---

[13]The average age of a menopausal woman in the United States is 51 years

3. How could we better address any challenges or new opportunities we have with the changes in her body?

Read and Consider

Read together Genesis 18:11-12 (ESV).

Now Abraham and Sarah were old, advanced in years. The way of women had ceased to be with Sarah. So Sarah laughed to herself, saying, "After I am worn out, and my lord is old, shall I have pleasure?"

Some versions translate the last sentence something like: "After I am old and my husband old, shall I have this pleasure?" But the original Hebrew words indicate that Sarah was describing the time she'd passed "the way of women," meaning a reproductive cycle, as feeling "worn out" and saying it wasn't conducive to pleasure. Menopause had made permanent her barrenness—without God's supernatural intervention—but it also wasn't working wonders for her sex life.

Were Abraham and Sarah still making love? We cannot say, though we hope they continued to experience physical intimacy. Yet a woman's changing body can negatively impact her experience. Symptoms of menopause often include vaginal dryness, hot flashes and night sweats, changes in libido, weight gain, sleep disruption, and/or mood swings. Any one of these can affect sexual intimacy, but dealing with several can prove particularly formidable.

Intentionally address these issues together and find ways to be supportive and intimate.

Touch and Pray

Our Lord, You created a window of opportunity for reproduction and a biological way for that window to close. We thank You for Your perfect design, but also recognize the brokenness of our world means that negative issues can arise surrounding menopause. Help us to meet those challenges together.

[Pray for the specifics you discussed.]

In the holy name of Jesus, Amen.

Go and Do

1. Individually list three benefits of a woman undergoing perimenopause or menopause. Then trade lists and talk about how you can find the positivity in this season of your marriage.

2. For one week, keep track of symptoms you notice in the wife that are, or could, be related to perimenopause or menopause. Becoming aware can help you both understand how these changes impact your lives as a whole and your marriage bed in particular.

Pillow Talk

Chapter 29
PREGNANCY AND SEX

Congratulations! You're expecting a baby. While this is a marvelous development for your family, it can also be a challenging one for your sexual intimacy. The physical changes a wife undergoes can impact your marriage bed in many ways, from availability to frequency to positions. How can you keep sexual intimacy alive and well throughout the pregnancy?

Ask and Listen

1. What specific challenges do we face at this stage of pregnancy?

2. What issues do you see in the future that we may need to address together?

3. What ideas do you have for us continuing to be sexually connected? How can we please and satisfy one another?

Read and Consider

Read together Psalm 127:3-5.

> *Children are a heritage from the Lord,*
> *offspring a reward from him.*
> *Like arrows in the hands of a warrior*
> *are children born in one's youth.*
> *Blessed is the man*
> *whose quiver is full of them.[14]*
> *They will not be put to shame*
> *when they contend with their opponents in court.*

God says that children are a blessing! But let's face it: they are also a challenge, even before they come into the world. The mother senses this life shift more intensely as her own body is invaded by a being with an inordinate amount of say on what she eats, when she sleeps, how she feels, and more. All of these factors can impact her sexuality.

Meanwhile, fathers have their own challenges, perhaps feeling new pressure about providing for his family, confusing feelings about seeing his wife as both a mom and a lover, and just working his way around her issues and her growing belly.

For the vast majority of couples, however, sexual intimacy is possible for most, if not all, of the pregnancy. You may need to be creative about timing, positions, and activities, but husband and wife should continue to enjoy one

---

[14]In the current climate of the Christian Quiverfill Movement, let me simply state that this verse is not a command from God to have unlimited children. We do not all have the same size quivers. Jacob had twelve sons to create the twelve tribes of Israel, yet Zechariah and Elizabeth had only one child—John the Baptist—yet what a difference their small family made! God can work through our families, whatever their size.

another's bodies and connect physically. Remember that the foundation of your family should be a devoted marriage.

Touch and Pray

Lord, thank You for this child and all the wonderful experiences that will come with expanding our family. Show us how to provide a solid foundation for our children with a healthy and holy marriage. Help us to never forget that we are not merely mom and dad to our children, but also lovers to one another.

[Pray for the challenges you discussed.]

In the name of Your Son, Amen.

Go and Do

1. Set up a sex encounter in which you kiss, touch, and pleasure one another *without* intercourse. Talk about all the many activities available to you in the marriage bed and how that experience informs the rest of your pregnancy and the time after baby comes.

2. Consult the website Christian Friendly Sex Positions for ideas on positions recommended during pregnancy. Talk about which ones appeal to you both and try them as needed or desired.

Pillow Talk

Chapter 30
SAYING NO TO SEX

The Bible instructs us not to "deprive one another" of sexual relations (1 Corinthians 7:3-5), but what does that actually mean? Are we ever permitted to say no to our spouse's sexual advances? Under what circumstances is a pass acceptable? And how can we handle those moments with love and grace?

Ask and Listen

1. Have you ever felt deprived of sexual intimacy in our marriage? If so, for what reason?[15]

2. What reasons should qualify as good ones for saying no to sex at a certain time?

3. If I need to turn down a sexual advance in a particular moment, what's the best way for me to do it without hurting you?

---

[15]Frequency is not the only cause of feeling deprived in the marriage bed.

Read and Consider

Read together Philippians 2:1-4.

> *Therefore if you have any encouragement from being
> united with Christ, if any comfort from his love, if
> any common sharing in the Spirit, if any tenderness
> and compassion, then make my joy complete by
> being like-minded, having the same love, being one
> in spirit and of one mind. Do nothing out of selfish
> ambition or vain conceit. Rather, in humility value
> others above yourselves, not looking to your own
> interests but each of you to the interests of the others.*

Yes, the Bible talks about not depriving one another. However, imagine that word "deprive" applied to physical hunger, rather than sexual hunger. Going without food for a long period of time is deprivation, but missing one meal isn't.

If your spouse needs to say no at a particular time—due to exhaustion, feeling unwell, or another good reason—tenderness, compassion, and "not looking to your own interests but each of you to the interests of the others" reminds us that we can accept a pass. However, it's easier to accept a single rejection when we know that a makeup date is coming soon. So the spouse who passes this time can offer a rain check for the following day or another time that will work better.

Give sexual intimacy its due attention, but don't worry if a single time doesn't work out like one spouse planned. The beauty of a long marriage is the opportunity to establish a pattern of lovemaking that makes up for any moments when things don't turn out as expected.

Touch and Pray

*God, we don't want to neglect our marriage bed,
but we recognize that a single missed opportunity will not deprive us of the intimacy You
designed for us to have. Help us to be tender,
compassionate, and loving—both in prioritizing regular lovemaking and also accepting a
pass if sex cannot happen at a particular time.*

[Pray for the challenges you discussed.]

In the name of our Lord and Savior, Amen.

Go and Do

1. Identifying circumstances that prevent you from feeling like making love can help you address or work around
obstacles, allowing you to say yes more often. Complete the
checklist and follow-up exercise at Appendix D on "What's
in the Way of Yes?"

2. Decide together how many passes are reasonable in a
single month, and then create/print rain check coupons in
the same number. You can find many templates online or
just make them by hand. Use your coupon to say no when
you feel you must, and in turn honor your spouse using the
rain check. Discuss how this system works for you two and
what it illuminated about the yeses and nos of your sexual
intimacy.

Pillow Talk

Chapter 31
EROGENOUS ZONES

Merriam-Webster defines *erogenous zone* as "a sensitive area on the body that causes sexual arousal when it is touched.[16]" Erogenous zones don't have to be at or even near genitalia, and they vary from person to person. One spouse might adore having their neck kissed, while another is aroused by having their bum squeezed. We cannot assume what turns us on will turn our spouse on, so it's important to find out where their erogenous zones are.

Ask and Listen

1. Which places on your body would you like me to touch or kiss?

2. How do you enjoy being touched or kissed there? What kind of movement, pressure, and progression do you find arousing?

---

[16]"Erogenous Zone." Merriam-Webster. Accessed September 24, 2018. https://www. merriam-webster.com/dictionary/erogenous zone.

3. Which places on your body or actions I've made or could make are a turn-off?

Read and Consider

Read together Song of Songs 7:6-9.

> *How beautiful you are and how pleasing,*
> *my love, with your delights!*
> *Your stature is like that of the palm,*
> *and your breasts like clusters of fruit.*
> *I said, "I will climb the palm tree;*
> *I will take hold of its fruit."*
> *May your breasts be like clusters of grapes on*
> *the vine, the fragrance of your breath like*
> *apples, and your mouth like the best wine.*

Breasts are mentioned a lot in Song of Songs, likely because they are a key erogenous zone for many husbands and wives—including this couple. What's intriguing is the way this husband seems in awe of his wife's erogenous zone. He appreciates its appearance, likens it to something delightful (clusters of fruit/grapes), and tells her just what he wants to do with that zone.

His concern is both for his arousal and for hers. Indeed, her answer after this passage is "May the wine go straight to my beloved, flowing gently over lips and teeth. I belong to my beloved, and his desire is for me" (Song of Songs 7:9-10). That sounds like a green flag!

These lovers mention many other parts of one another's bodies and how much they enjoy them. Likewise, explore your spouse's body, ask how you can arouse your beloved, and then cater to their erogenous zones with the awe and delight they deserve.

Touch and Pray

Our Creator, You have given our bodies, and specifically our skin, the ability to respond in many ways to touch. We thank You for this gift and ask for Your guidance in using it wisely in our marriage bed. Be with us as we look on one another's bodies with delight and touch those places that arouse each of us.

[Pray about the desires you discussed.]

In and through Jesus we pray, Amen.

Go and Do

1. Using a Sharpie marker, temporary tattoos, body paint, or even chocolate syrup, number the areas on your body where you'd like special attention during foreplay. Have your spouse follow the sequence you laid out, stopping at each location to deliver the kind of touch and kissing you desire.

2. With a dice template (you can find many online), create your own dice for each spouse with their six favorite erogenous zones. Using a timer, play a game in which you take turns rolling your spouse's dice, reading the

erogenous zone that comes up, and spending an agreed amount of time touching and kissing that area.

Chapter 32
MASTURBATION

Let's discuss a touchy subject, masturbation. (Did you catch the joke?) Ask a panel of Christians whether masturbation is okay or not, and you'll get a wide range of answers.[17] While cases can be made for and against, what matters most is how you as a couple decide to address masturbation. Will it be off-limits? Allowed? Restricted? What standard do you wish to apply in your marriage?

Ask and Listen

1. When do you think masturbation is okay, and when it is not okay? Why?

2. Have you ever masturbated when I didn't know about it? If so, why?

3. How would you like masturbation to be addressed in our marriage? What concerns do you have?

---

[17]For my take based primarily on the Bible, go to https://hotholyhumorous.com/2012/09/masturbation-hands-on-or-hands-off/.

Read and Consider

Read together Colossians 3:9-10.

Do not lie to each other, since you have taken
off your old self with its practices and have
put on the new self, which is being renewed
in knowledge in the image of its Creator.

Let's address the two Bible passages that some believers say forbid masturbation in all its forms. First, Genesis 38 tells the story of Onan, who spilled his seed on the ground; however, he wasn't engaging in masturbation but rather withdrawing before ejaculation. His sin was pursuing selfish pleasure with a widow while forsaking his legal duty to provide his brother an heir. Second, in 2 Timothy 3, Paul references marks of the last days, including that people will be "lovers of themselves," and someone, somewhere decided that masturbation was that self-love—despite this passage having nothing to do with sex. A plain reading that people like themselves more than they like God makes a whole lot more sense.

Thus, we don't have a straight yes or no to masturbation from the Word of God. What we do have are clear principles about not being selfish and pursuing the best interests of others. It's possible to imagine scenarios in which masturbation could benefit the marriage and ones in which it wouldn't. For example, a spouse touching themselves during sex could be mutually pleasurable and intimate, while masturbating alone and refusing your spouse's sexual advances removes the opportunity for connection.

But from the scripture above, we know that we should

be honest with each other in marriage. So if masturbating is something you must hide from your spouse, you probably shouldn't be doing it. Talk about the issue and decide together about how you'll handle masturbation.

Touch and Pray

God, You created sex for marriage and
our sexual energy should be focused on one
another, not merely our own self-pleasure.
Show us how to pursue this goal well.

[Pray about the issues you discussed.]

In Jesus' holy name, Amen.

Go and Do

1. Write a letter for yourself detailing your past experiences with masturbation—what you were taught about it, whether you did it, how you did it, whether problematic imagery was part of it, what your feelings were about it, and what the results of your choices were. Based on your past, consider what you should change about your approach in the future. (If you want, you may trade letters, but you may also keep them private.)

2. One reason to engage in masturbation is to explore for yourself how you like to be touched, which is good information for your spouse to have. If you're comfortable with this idea, take turns in bed together touching yourself while the spouse watches to see what you do, so they can emulate it later with their own hand.

Chapter 33
SEXUAL HARASSMENT

In case you didn't notice, a little thing happened in 2018 called #MeToo. Whether you consider this movement, on balance, a positive or negative development, it had the effect of bringing to many people's minds the sexual harassment they'd experienced. Let's take a look at how sexual harassment may have impacted the physical intimacy in your marriage.

Ask and Listen

1. Have you been sexually harassed? What happened, and how did it make you feel?

2. How do you define sexual harassment? Give examples of what is or is not sexual harassment to you.

3. How has your experience with sexual harassment affected your view of your body or sexuality as a whole?

Read and Consider

Read Ruth 2:5-9 together.

Boaz asked the overseer of his harvesters, "Who does that young woman belong to?" The overseer replied, "She is the Moabite who came back from Moab with Naomi. She said, 'Please let me glean and gather among the sheaves behind the harvesters.' She came into the field and has remained here from morning till now, except for a short rest in the shelter." So Boaz said to Ruth, "My daughter, listen to me. Don't go and glean in another field and don't go away from here. Stay here with the women who work for me. Watch the field where the men are harvesting, and follow along after the women. I have told the men not to lay a hand on you. And whenever you are thirsty, go and get a drink from the water jars the men have filled."

Sexual harassment has been around for a very long time. When Boaz came upon Ruth gleaning in his fields, he understood the risk she faced. He'd likely seen other women receive sexual advances or unwanted touching or inappropriate comments.

Surely these women felt anxiety while they performed tasks necessary to feed their families, but Boaz stepped up and provided Ruth protection. He told the male harvesters to leave her alone. We should follow this example of protecting people in lesser positions from those who might prey upon them in the workplace or elsewhere.

A husband in particular can be a strong influence in demonstrating to his wife respect and and safety.

Although sexual harassment definitely happens to men as well.[18]

Touch and Pray

God, in this broken world, selfish people will try to take advantage of others. Help us to see sexual harassment for what it is, to pursue justice wherever possible, and to support one another fully. Lord, keep our experiences with sexual harassment from weakening our desire for or commitment to healthy and holy sexual intimacy in the marriage bed.

[Pray about the experiences you discussed.]

We know full justice is in Your hands. In the name of Jesus we pray, Amen.

Go and Do

1. Write a letter apologizing for any times you sexually harassed someone. This letter is not to send to those you mistreated, but to open your eyes to how you may have intentionally or unintentionally caused someone harm. Bring these concerns before God and ask for His forgiveness.

2. Talk about how you as a couple would deal with sexual harassment if it happened to one of you. What steps would you take to protect yourselves and hold the perpetrator responsible?

---

[18]For an example of a man being sexually harassed, read Genesis 39:6-10, in which his employer's wife relentlessly pursues Joseph, then accused him of maltreatment.

Pillow Talk

Chapter 34
SEXUAL BAGGAGE

Sexual baggage refers to ideas or experiences that create a burden or obstacle to embracing the sexual intimacy God desires you to have. This includes a lot of issues, from body image to bad teaching to past promiscuity to sexual abuse.[19] Whatever feels like a barrier keeping you from enjoying sexual intimacy could be labeled baggage.

Ask and Listen

1. What ideas or experiences have you had that feel like sexual baggage?

2. What ideas or experiences do you believe might be sexual baggage for me?

3. How can I help you address your sexual baggage so that we can enjoy our sexual intimacy more?

---

[19]If you experienced abuse, you may wish to pause and read the chapter that addresses Past Sexual Abuse.

Read and Consider

Read together 2 Corinthians 5:16-19.

So from now on we regard no one from a worldly point of view. Though we once regarded Christ in this way, we do so no longer. Therefore, if anyone is in Christ, the new creation has come: The old has gone, the new is here! All this is from God, who reconciled us to himself through Christ and gave us the ministry of reconciliation: that God was reconciling the world to himself in Christ, not counting people's sins against them. And he has committed to us the message of reconciliation.

God's desire is that we be reconciled to Him, and to the life He wants to give us. Regardless of its origin, any baggage we hang onto can hold us back from embracing what God intends us to have. We need to let go.

Of course this isn't a flip of the switch, but a process. A couple of chapters earlier in 2 Corinthians, the apostle Paul says, "And we all, who with unveiled faces contemplate the Lord's glory, are being transformed into his image with ever-increasing glory, which comes from the Lord, who is the Spirit" (3:18). We're being transformed, but not quite there yet.

What matters is taking steps in the right direction. Do you want to let go of that baggage? Do you desire to be reconciled to God's plan for sexual intimacy? Are you ready to take the first steps? God has something much better for you to hang onto—His precious gift of physical intimacy in the marriage bed.

Touch and Pray

Lord, we feel the heaviness of our sexual baggage weighing us down and keeping us from embracing Your gift of sexual intimacy as we should. Satan has tried to twist Your blessing and make it into a curse. Help us to fight against these obstacles with truth, perseverance, and one another's support.

[Pray about the specific sexual baggage you each have.]

We thank you for Jesus, who promised His rest from our burdens [Matthew 11:28], and pray in His name, Amen.

Go and Do

1. Write down one idea you've believed about sex that you logically know is not God's design for sex in marriage. Now write down the truth about sex as God created it. In the next week, review each of those, becoming more aware of the falsehood and practicing how you can replace it with the truth. Variation: Do this with and for each other, asking your spouse to also gently remind you of the truth you need to be reconciled to.

2. List three ways you have grown in your viewpoint about sex since you got married, or since you began this book together. Talk with each other about the progress you've made, recognizing that you have already taken positive steps

and can continue to let go of your baggage and discover God's goodness for your marriage bed.

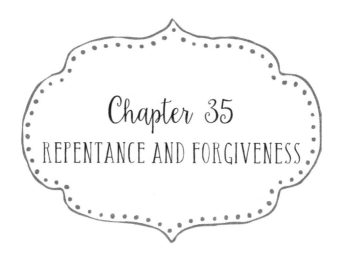

Chapter 35
REPENTANCE AND FORGIVENESS

Somewhere in the course of our sexual intimacy, we mess up. We pursue our own selfish pleasures more than our spouse's satisfaction, we refuse or neglect sexual intimacy, we overlook romance and/or foreplay, we let sexual baggage from our past interfere with our marriage bed in the present. Since we're not perfect, we let our spouse down. And we are let down by our spouse. It can become easy, even comfortable, to hold onto bitterness over the sins and slights of our mate. But it isn't a healthy path for marital intimacy.

Ask and Listen

1. When it comes to our sex life, how have I hurt you? What have I done that has caused you emotional pain?

2. Where do you feel that you've let me down?

3. What would an apology look like to you? What words or actions would help you believe that I don't want to hurt you?

Read and Consider

Read together Ephesians 4:31-32.

*Get rid of all bitterness, rage and anger, brawling
and slander, along with every form of malice. Be
kind and compassionate to one another, forgiving
each other, just as in Christ God forgave you.*

A proverb of unknown origin states, "Never ruin an
apology with an excuse." And yet, too often we don't accept
responsibility for hurting our spouse. We make excuses.

Even unintentional slights can bring emotional pain to
the one we love. We should listen to how our spouse feels
and be quick to apologize when we have injured them.
Afterward, determine how you can repent—that is, change
what you're doing to avoid or lessen hurts in the future.

In turn, the above passage reminds us to let go of bitterness and forgive one another. Full forgiveness can take time,
as we remind ourselves of the overall goodness of our spouse,
the love we know they feel for us, and our mutual desire to
pursue holiness and happiness.

But holding onto hurts impedes our willingness to be
fully present in the marriage bed. Is it time to let go of bitterness you've been holding onto?

Touch and Pray

*God, if You held our sins over us and dealt
with us in bitterness, we would have no hope.
Instead, You've shown again and again that
You forgive and reconcile with those who confess and repent. Give us the humility to confess
and repent when we have wronged one another
and the grace to forgive and reconcile.*

[Pray about the hurts you discussed before.]

*We thank You for the perfect sacrifice of
Your Son and pray in His name, Amen.*

Go and Do

1. Write a letter to your spouse apologizing for what
you feel you've done wrong in the past regarding sex
in your marriage and/or acknowledging what they feel
you've done wrong. Explain how you want them to feel
instead, reassuring them of your love, and outline specific steps you'll take to make things better.

2. Write a letter to your spouse forgiving them for how
they've hurt you in the past. If you know the process
will take time, acknowledge that fact and explain how
you plan to move in the right direction. Include any
requests you have for your spouse in helping you overcome your hurt and choosing forgiveness instead. To
remind yourself and your spouse, sign the letter with

this phrase from 1 Corinthians 13:5: "Love keeps no record of wrongs."

Chapter 36
REACHING CLIMAX

An orgasm is "a series of muscle contractions in the genital region that is accompanied by sudden release of endorphins."[20] But that description hardly covers the way it feels to have one. As the apex of pleasure, orgasm is an important aspect of sexual intimacy—but not one all spouses experience as they should.

Ask and Listen

1. How often do you experience orgasm when we make love?[21]

2. How does it feel when you to reach orgasm, and/or how does it feel when you don't reach orgasm?

3. Do you believe I prioritize your orgasm enough? Why or why not?

---

[20] "Definition of Orgasm." MedicineNet. Accessed November 08, 2018. https://www.medicinenet.com/script/main/art.asp?articlekey=11783.

[21] If you've been "faking it," now is the time to come clean—explaining why you believed pretending was a good idea and why you now want to pursue vulnerability and authenticity in the marriage bed.

Read and Consider

Read together Song of Songs 4:16-5:1 (HCSB).

She: *Awaken, north wind—*
come, south wind.
Blow on my garden,
and spread the fragrance of its spices.
Let my love come to his garden
and eat its choicest fruits.

He: *I have come to my garden*
my sister, my bride.
I gather my myrrh with my spices.
I eat my honeycomb with my honey.
I drink my wine with my milk.

Narrator: *Eat, friends!*
Drink, be intoxicated with love!

Some versions translate that last line as "drink your fill" or "drink deeply," but the original Hebrew word is more in line with intoxication—that is, getting drunk on love. Although moderation is often the prescribed path for believers, when it comes to the marriage bed, God gives us not only permission but encouragement to gather as much pleasure as we'd like. He gifted us with the capacity to experience orgasm and wants us to embrace that pinnacle of pleasure.

For the husband, reaching climax is less likely to be a struggle, but this can change as his body ages and greater and longer stimulation is required to achieve climax. For the wife, orgasm can range anywhere from easy to elusive, as the causes for reaching that peak are more varied and complicated. But one thing we know—the clitoris has no other purpose than to provide a wife pleasure and get her to orgasm. So clearly God values orgasm for both spouses.

Although orgasm may not be possible every time, it's worth prioritizing and pursuing.[22]

Touch and Pray

Heavenly Father, You could have made sex a purely reproductive act, but in Your generosity, You designed it to provide immense pleasure as well. Help us to experience all You created our bodies to experience, including climax.

[Pray for the challenges or goals you discussed.]

In Your Son's holy name, Amen.

Do and Do

1. Together visit Appendix E to learn more about arousal and orgasm. Then discuss your favorite facts and why you found that tidbit interesting.

---

[22]If orgasm has been hard for you to reach, wives, my book, *Hot, Holy, and Humorous: Sex in Marriage by God's Design*, has specific tips on helping you achieve that elusive peak of pleasure.

2. Plan a sexual encounter in which you focus on one spouse's pleasure. Don't worry, you'll be taking turns. Allow the one receiving to give direction and feedback on what feels good, through words, noises, or moving the other's hand. If the receiver can reach orgasm, great. If not, they should still decide how long to go before moving onto other activities. Use this as a learning experience for what provides the most pleasure to your spouse.

Chapter 37
WHAT ARE YOU WEARING?

"What are you wearing?" It's a question lovers have flirtatiously asked one another in texts, phone conversations, and before that, handwritten letters. Why does this question matter? Because we like to envision our beloved dressed to impress—even, or most especially, in the bedroom.

Ask and Listen

1. What do you like to wear to bed and why?

2. What do you like to see me wear to bed and why?

3. How does what we wear affect our arousal and sexual frequency?

Read and Consider

Read together Isaiah 61:10.

I delight greatly in the Lord;
my soul rejoices in my God.
For he has clothed me with garments of salvation
and arrayed me in a robe of his righteousness,
as a bridegroom adorns his head like a priest,
and as a bride adorns herself with her jewels.

In this chapter, Isaiah prophesies the restoration of God's people and foreshadows the coming of Christ. As part of this proclamation, Isaiah refers to the practice of bride and bridegroom putting on their Sunday best for their wedding. Later in Revelation 21:2, the apostle John confirms this practice: "I saw the Holy City, the new Jerusalem, coming down out of heaven from God, prepared as a bride beautifully dressed for her husband."

Just as we did for our wedding, we should prepare ourselves for one another in the marriage bed. We may not expend the same care and attention that we did for the monumental event of exchanging vows, but attending to our appearance and choosing something pleasing to wear are small steps we can take to express the importance of our spouse and our desire for ongoing intimacy.

Touch and Pray

*Our Father, we recognize that what we wear
is nowhere near as important as who we are.
Yet clothing, or the lack of it, can help us feel
more sexually confident or engaged in the marriage bed. Our choices of what to wear can
strengthen our intimacy by helping to arouse
and please one another. Help us to come to
unity on how we will address this issue.*

*[Pray about the approach to cloth-
ing you discussed together.]*

In the name of our bridegroom Jesus, Amen.

Go and Do

1. Based on your spouse's answer to what they'd like you
to wear, choose an outfit from your existing wardrobe or
purchase one. You don't need to move from what you're
comfortable wearing all the way to what he/she desires to
see you in, but take a step in that direction. Move closer
to what your spouse appreciates. Then wear it to bed.

2. Compliment your spouse's appearance at least twice
this week. If necessary, create a reminder on your calendar to make sure you do it. Be honest and specific
about what you find attractive in your mate. Bonus:
Compliment your spouse once when they're dressed for
bed and once when they're fully clothed.

Pillow Talk

Chapter 38
HAVING THE TALK WITH OUR KIDS

Whether you have kids now, will have kids, or only encounter other people's kids, you're likely to have some opportunity to impress upon the younger generation your view of sex. Of course, parents have a special responsibility to teach their children about God's desire for our lives, including sexuality.

Ask and Listen

1. What did your parents tell you about sex?

2. Where else did you learn about sex, and what messages were part of that learning?

3. What do you want our children to know about sex?

Read and Consider

Read together Proverbs 5:15-20.

> *Drink water from your own cistern,*
> *running water from your own well.*
> *Should your springs overflow in the streets,*
> *your streams of water in the public squares?*
> *Let them be yours alone,*
> *never to be shared with strangers.*
> *May your fountain be blessed,*
> *and may you rejoice in the wife of your youth.*
> *A loving doe, a graceful deer—*
> *may her breasts satisfy you always,*
> *may you ever be intoxicated with her love.*
> *Why, my son, be intoxicated*
> *with another man's wife?*
> *Why embrace the bosom of a wayward woman?*

This instruction was delivered from a father to his son. The father establishes himself as one with wisdom on this subject, spending this chapter and the next advising his son in this area.

Perhaps it's surprising how frank this parent was. But clearly this father was more concerned with his child receiving the right messages about sex than the embarrassment they might experience from this conversation.

Meanwhile, our children are also bombarded with messages about sex that don't comply with God's design. As parents and Christians, we have the responsibility to share God's truth about this sensitive yet significant issue. It doesn't matter whether we always did it right ourselves; we now have wisdom they need to hear. Our children deserve adults who demonstrate that we know, we care, and we can handle their questions.

Touch and Pray

God, we recognize our responsibility to teach children about sex, but we also feel ill-equipped at times to provide all the information and guidance we want to give. Help us to overcome any awkwardness and to speak tenderly yet candidly about Your design for sexuality and the blessings of sex in marriage. Above all, help us to model healthy and holy sexual intimacy, through the hints they see of our physical connection.

[Pray about any obstacles or opportunities you have in addressing this topic.]

We pray in Your Son's name, Amen.

Go and Do

1. Read Appendix F: Talking to Your Kids about Sex and discuss the points. Where are you in this process?

2. If it's time to open up a conversation, decide together when you'll sit down and chat with your child. Remember that young children just need basics, older children need an opportunity to ask questions, and teenagers need you to listen to where they are and ask follow-up questions to shape their thinking.

Pillow Talk

Chapter 39
IS LUSTING GOOD OR BAD?

Lust has a bad reputation in the Christian world. This word is almost always used in a negative way, referring to sexual desire we shouldn't have. But what really constitutes lust? Is it noticing? Looking too long? Dwelling on a visual? And is that desire always bad? The topic of lust is definitively worth a marital discussion.

Ask and Listen

1. What do you think it means to lust? What counts as lusting and what doesn't?

2. How does my definition affect you? How do you feel about it?

3. How is your sexual desire for me different from what you feel about anyone else?

Read and Consider

Read together Matthew 5:27-28.

"You have heard that it was said, 'You shall not commit adultery.' But I tell you that anyone who looks at a woman lustfully has already committed adultery with her in his heart."

The Greek word for lust in this verse is *epithumeó*, which merely refers to a strong desire. Indeed, this same word, and its sister word *epithumia*, are used at the Passover Supper with Jesus, when He says, "I have *eagerly desired* to eat this Passover with you before I suffer."

The problem with *epithumeó* occurs when our strong desire is in conflict with what God intends for us to have—such as sexual thoughts about someone who isn't our spouse. That's always labeled as wrong.

However, it's both healthy and holy to have this *epithumeó*, or strong desire, for your spouse. Marriage is the sacred setting for sexual longing. We must learn to turn away from lusts that take sexual focus away from our spouse and return our longing to where God intends it to be—on the beloved spouse He has blessed you with.

Touch and Pray

Our God, although we may be aware of others who are attractive or sexually appealing, we want our longings to be focused on one another. Help us to resist the temptation to lust after others, knowing that such action counts as adultery in our hearts. Turn our eyes and our minds instead to one another, so that our sexual desire is aroused, nurtured, and satisfied within our marriage.

In Jesus we pray, Amen.

Go and Do

1. Think about the shows you watch, books you read, media you consume. Do any of these tempt you to lust after others? If so, make the decision to seek out healthier choices. In today's world, you have an ample number of options.

2. Make extra efforts this week to express to your spouse how much you desire them and them alone. Speak up, text, leave notes, or just embrace more often, but make it clear to your spouse that you only have eyes for them.

Pillow Talk

Chapter 40
SEXUAL SEASONS

Just when you think you've got it all worked out, life changes. It happens in every area of our lives, doesn't it? Our children grow up, job responsibilities shift, technology advances, and our marriages enter a new season. Since we also change and grow through the years, we must continue to nurture our marriage and sexual intimacy—knowing our next season won't look like the last one. But, with God's help, it can be even more intimate.

Ask and Listen

1. Which season would you compare our marriage to—spring, summer, fall, winter—and why?

2. How do you believe we've changed in the course of our marriage, especially when it comes to sex?

3. What do you think we can do to make this season better than the last one?

Read and Consider

Read together Song of Songs 2:11-13.

"See! The winter is past;
the rains are over and gone.
Flowers appear on the earth;
the season of singing has come,
the cooing of doves
is heard in our land.
The fig tree forms its early fruit;
the blossoming vines spread their fragrance.
Arise, come, my darling;
my beautiful one, come with me."

Even the lovers in Song of Songs understood some seasons might be more amenable to romance and intimacy than others. While true of our weather, it's also true of marriages in general. Some seasons lend themselves to frequent lovemaking or adventurous positions or sex in the afternoon, but we can also experience dry spells now and again.

One clear benefit of God's design for sex in marriage is that our physical intimacy isn't comprised of a single encounter or a brief period of time, but rather a lifetime of getting to know one another, investing in each other's hearts and bodies, and forming a bond like no other.

Compassion for each other and commitment to the marriage bed are essential in dealing with our seasons of sexual intimacy. While sexual intimacy should never be neglected, aspects may need to be paused or altered. Physical or relational obstacles may need to be addressed. Tactics and techniques may need to be revisited.

Touch and Pray

God, You are the creator of seasons and the bringer of true change. We ask You to change us day after day to become more like You, in our lives and in our marriage. Help us weather other changes and seasons of life with love, compassion, and hope for the future.

[Pray for the season you're in, or the one to come.]

In our blessed Savior's name, Amen.

Go and Do

1. If you have faced a recent challenge to your marriage bed, due to physical, emotional, or relational changes, consider what options you have to address it. If you need to have a candid conversation with your spouse, have it. If you need to make an appointment with a physician or a counselor, do it this week. If you need other resources, research what you need and then make contact. Take one important step toward a season of better sexual intimacy.

2. Celebrate the season you're in! List three positives about being in the season of marriage you believe you're in. What benefits are there to where you are now, and how will they lead to greater intimacy in the future? Thank God for those positives.

Pillow Talk

Addressing
Specific Issues

In this section, we address three specific issues that require additional attention. If you have had past sexual abuse, used porn, or experienced performance challenges (for him), be sure to read that particular chapter. For the sake of your marriage and its sexual intimacy, you must take action to heal from these struggles.

Invite the support of your spouse as well. Being one flesh in marriage means all sexual problems are a *we* problem—affecting the marriage bed for both of you.

Each of these issues may require external help, through a licensed therapist. The final chapter in this section on choosing a counselor will help you navigate that process.

Past Sexual Abuse

Spouses who have been sexually harassed, assaulted, and abused have a more difficult time embracing God's gift of intimacy. It's imperative that they go through a process of recovery. Most traumatic experiences require external help.

Find a support group, a trauma counselor, a trusted pastor, and/or a fellow-survivor mentor. Resources like Dan Allender's book, *The Wounded Heart*, and RAINN (Rape, Abuse & Incest National Network) can help you work through the residual pain.

Be sure to discuss your "triggers" with your spouse; that is, what stimuli trigger feelings related to the trauma you experienced. For example, a husband grabbing his wife's butt without warning—even with loving intent—can trigger feelings reminiscent of her bad experience, like loss of control, personal violation, and objectification. Talk out what actions make you feel unsafe and how you can increase your sense of security with one another.

Be patient and support each other as you address these issues. They can be overcome, but it takes time and intentionality. You may also experience more emotional pain in the short-term as buried memories are brought to light, but the health of your heart and your marriage bed will be the worth the journey.

5 Reasons to Stop Using Porn

If you're using pornography, here are five good reasons why it's time to stop:

1. It messes with your brain. Habitual porn use retrains your brain to use imagery as the primary source of sexual pleasure, to desire extreme variety and even cruelty, and to objectify potential partners.[23] A diet of porn can impair one's ability to perform and connect with a real woman. This condition is called Porn-Induced Erectile Dysfunction (PIED), and more doctors are seeing erectile problems with younger men who have engaged with porn.

Experts theorize that these men are desensitized to normal sexual stimuli and require a level of imagery, intensity, and novelty that isn't real-life. Thankfully, some of these men are speaking up against the very activity they used to frequently pursue, warning of the dangers and consequences of consuming pornography.

2. It makes real sex less satisfying. Pornography focuses on the physical aspect and contains many myths about sex. Users, therefore, become less satisfied with the real thing—expecting sex to look like what they see on screen. Their disappointment can lead to seeking greater and greater highs, all the while missing that true sexual fulfillment isn't all about increasing your physical pleasure quota. Rather, sex involves a real person (your spouse); includes

---

[23]See Struthers, William M. *Wired for Intimacy: How Pornography Hijacks the Male Brain*. Downers Grove, IL: InterVarsity Press, 2009; also Gary Wilson "The Great Porn Experiment," May 16, 2012, Glasgow, Tedx video, 16:28, https://youtu.be/wSF82AwSDiU.

mental, emotional, and spiritual aspects; and satisfies when it represents a commitment and relational intimacy.

Consider prominent marriage and relationship researchers John and Julie Gottman of the Gottman Institute, who were previously proponents of using porn to increase intimacy in relationships. Based on various studies, they changed their minds and concluded that "use of pornography by one partner leads the couple to have far less sex and ultimately reduces relationship satisfaction."[24]

3. It encourages abuse. If you're viewing porn, you need to think carefully about how your consumer habits influence those who put out the product. A lot of abuse occurs in the porn industry, and our societal support has a detrimental effect on those involved. The more people who watch porn, the more porn actors will be injured, contract sexual diseases, and take drugs to numb their senses.

Also, the prevalence of minors being used for porn has greatly increased. Sex traffickers are more than willing to use their victims for this purpose. Although the vast majority of people would cringe at the idea of involving children in the making of porn, it happens whether or not the larger population is aware, due to high demand and ease of anonymity.

4. It dishonors your spouse. When you gaze longingly, lustfully, sexually at others, you dishonor your spouse. You send a message that they aren't enough to arouse and satisfy your sexual desire. I'm not talking about a stray thought of a gorgeous person passing you by on the street, but the

---

[24]John, and Julie Gottman. "An Open Letter on Porn." The Gottman Institute. April 09, 2018. Accessed November 24, 2018. https://www.gottman.com/blog/an-open-letter-on-porn/.

dwelling of your mind on someone else and using that to titillate your sex drive. Porn is definitely in the category of allowing someone besides your spouse to arouse you sexually. And what does that communicate to him or her?

Frankly, most of us have enough built-in insecurities that having to compete for attention with a porn star is a big ol' slap-in-the-face. Your spouse should instead be reassured of your focus and love and commitment to them, and them alone.

5. It is a sin. If we go looking for a commandment that simply says, "Thou shalt not view pornography," you'd be right to say it doesn't exist. But short of an outright statement like that, the Bible can't get much clearer that pornography is not God's intention for sexuality. So let's take an honest, no-excuses approach to whether porn is sinful.

"But I tell you that anyone who looks at a woman lustfully has already committed adultery with her in his heart" (Matthew 5:28).

"Marriage should be honored by all, and the marriage bed kept pure, for God will judge the adulterer and all the sexually immoral" (Hebrews 13:4).

"I made a covenant with my eyes not to look lustfully at a young woman. For what is our lot from God above, our heritage from the Almighty on high? Is it not ruin for the wicked, disaster for those who do wrong? Does he not see my ways and count my every step?" (Job 31:1-4).

"Put to death, therefore, whatever belongs to your earthly nature: sexual immorality, impurity, lust, evil desires and greed, which is idolatry" (Colossians 3:5).

That's just a sampling.

Moreover, many scriptures talk about guarding our hearts and our minds so that we remained focused on the things of God. Yes, the "things of God" include sex, with your spouse as He designed. But involving a third party, even in the form of an image, detours from His path. Pornography is simply wrong.

Sadly, many people approach this subject with a "what can I get away with?" attitude—wanting to know how far they can go before crossing some imaginary line. The better question is: How can I honor God with my sexuality? Then seek that higher goal.

If you experience difficulty in stopping, please get help. It does not show weakness but rather courage to reach out for the assistance you need. Local resources can give you more personalized attention, but there are great online ministries as well:

XXXChurch helps both men and women break porn habits, overcome shame, and adopt a healthy view of sex. They also offer online small groups for those struggling, their spouses, and specifically pastors.

Dirty Girls Ministries aims to provide help, hope, and healing for women struggling with pornography and sexual addiction.

Covenant Eyes is an internet accountability service that helps people overcome porn habits by monitoring online activity and providing reports to an accountability partner.

View porn as an attack on your soul and your marriage, and do not let the enemy win. Together, as a couple, fight for healthy and holy sexuality.

Performance Challenges for Him

During sex, your penis has two main jobs: get hard, shoot semen. That's really it. Any other tricks it performs—whatever those might be—are bonuses.

And yet, sometimes Junior doesn't show up to the job with all the fervor you expect. You could be mentally excited by the sight of your naked wife, the prospect of sexual pleasure, the desire for physical release, and yet your penis won't get or keep an erection or you can't seem to reach climax.

Such issues are likely to crop up from time to time with middle-aged to elderly men, simply because our bodies atrophy as we age. We should be no more surprised that a penis gets a periodic glitch than we are when a joint does the same.

However, the problem has increased in recent years with young men, often attributable to the prevalence of porn use that trains the body to be aroused by imagery and self-stimulation more than sexual touch and interaction.

How you address the issue depends on its cause. The first order of business is heading to the doctor. Yes, that one—that doctor you've been avoiding for far too long. Even if you think you can live just fine without consistent erections and climaxes, erectile dysfunction has been linked to such health issues as heart disease and diabetes. Your issue could be a harbinger of bigger problems, so get a checkup and discuss Junior with Doctor. If the doctor deems the problem to be physiological, it can addressed in the same way—with diet, medication, or therapy.

Now if porn has been a prominent part of your sexual experiences, make sure you read the prior chapter on pornography. And in addition to stopping porn, you should also discontinue any masturbation (at least for the time being) and retrain your brain to be turned on by your wife. You may need to consult with a counselor who can deal both with building relational connection and sensate focus therapy, an expert-guided process by which you can recalibrate to arousal in the moment.

What if the issue is past sexual abuse? A number of men are walking around with a deep secret they've never told anyone, or maybe they have told someone but haven't addressed the lingering pain. Sexual abuse can cause performance difficulties, and the answer is to address the trauma you experienced. Go read the chapter on Past Sexual Abuse for more information.

And some husbands simply have difficulty performing because you were taught, in one way or another, that sex is bad. Some men experience guilt over sexual arousal based on erroneous teaching they received that sex is dirty, purely physical, unspiritual, or selfish. Hopefully, this book helps you move beyond those messages, but if this remains a challenge, write down the subconscious messages you have embraced, then write the truth about God's desire for your marriage bed and rehearse those answers. When guilt takes hold, remind yourself of God's goodness and generosity toward your sex life. Slowly but surely, you will embrace a holy and healthy view of sexual intimacy.

If none of these work, see a counselor. Either the marriage relationship itself or your own issues could be hindering progress. Talk it out with someone who can hear your personal story and make suggestions for what route to take.

Choosing and Working with a Counselor

If I had ten bucks for each time someone told me they tried counseling and it didn't work, I'd be on vacation in Italy right now. So if you're skeptical about going to counseling, I get it. Sometimes the client has a bad experience.

But neither do you like every doctor, dentist, mechanic, repairman, or hairstylist you've visited. Some worked out, some didn't. Counseling is the same in that you need to find the right expert.

How do you locate a quality counselor and work with them to address your particular issues?

Word of mouth. Do you know anyone who came back from the brink with the help of a counselor? You might without even knowing that you do. Ask trusted people who they recommend for counseling, and you may be surprised to discover that close friends have good suggestions. Just like any other service, word of mouth could be the best way to identify whether a counselor is worth your time.

Search online. Run an online search for counselors in your area and comb through the list for those who come from a Christian perspective. Secular counselors in the area of sex often suggest activities opposed God's teaching, so look instead for someone who honors your faith. Additionally, the American Association of Christian Counselors and the American Board of Christian Sex Therapists have databases you can search.

Check credentials. What degrees, certifications, and training do they have? Make sure whatever they cite is legitimate, which you can usually verify with a quick Google search. Some certifications are merely a matter of paying a fee and completing little if any coursework, while others involve extensive education. To help you out, here are some common US degrees and licensures: psychologist (PhD or PsyD in psychology), psychiatrist (MD or DO with residency training), licensed professional counselor (LPC), licensed marriage and family therapist (LMFT), licensed clinical social worker (LCSW). Professional associations also award certifications. Just make sure the counselor is credentialed and their practice governed by a board.

Interview the counselor. In your first phone call or meeting, ask questions about how the counselor approaches people and issues, what theories or models or resources they regularly employ, how long and how often they tend to see clients, and what if any outside tasks the client is expected to complete. How you view their answers is often personal prerogative, because a counselor could be great for Client A and not a good match for Client B.

However, their message should be consistent with Scripture, they should prioritize both the individual and their marriage, and they should give clients some kind of "homework." Epiphanies within a session can be helpful, but for lasting progress, you need to apply what you learn in therapy to real life.

Be honest. Your counselor cannot help you if you don't tell them what's going on. Withholding information can hinder your healing and recovery. Licensed counselors are legally bound to maintain your confidentiality, with very few exceptions, such as when they believe a client is a danger to himself or others. So go ahead and dump it all out there and see if they can help you sort it out.

Be willing to put forth effort. It's ever-so-tempting to walk into a counseling session looking simply for reassurance, sympathy, and/or justification. Counselors are not strangers to statements like, "I only look at porn because my spouse won't give me the sex I need" or "I was abused as a child, so my spouse shouldn't expect me to have sex." But even when struggles are reasonable given your situation, they are causing problems. If you can heal from them, why wouldn't you do that for yourself and for your marriage?

Be willing to challenge your thoughts and behaviors, consider new points of view, adopt better practices. You shouldn't be forced or pressured, but you also shouldn't be a stony resistance sitting on the therapy couch. Open yourself up to making changes that will eventually improve your life, your marriage, and your sexual intimacy.

If at first you don't succeed… It can be frustrating to go through two, four, or six sessions of therapy and then have to let go, but if you're not learning and improving, find someone else. You wouldn't go back to the same mechanic over and over and over if they couldn't fix your car, so why do that with your life and your marriage?

Now don't quit simply because you don't *feel* better. Unfortunately, therapy can be like closet cleaning, where things get messier before they get better. But if you feel stagnant, that's a signal that you and your counselor may not be a good match. Consider starting over with someone else. Don't give up on counseling, just on this particular attempt.

For those who don't have local options, look into online coaching. Some therapists you can find through the American Association of Christian Counselors or American Board of Christian Sex Therapists offer online services.

APPENDIX A
HOW WELL DO YOU KNOW YOUR SPOUSE?

Each of you should complete this 10-question quiz separately and privately. Fill in the blanks with what you believe is the right answer for your spouse. Then trade sheets and talk about your answers.[25]

1. My spouse likes his/her coffee (or tea) made with

_____

_____

_____.

2. My spouse's favorite hobby or activity is _____

_____

_____.

3. My spouse's idea of a perfect date is _____

_____

_____.

4. My spouse's favorite holiday is _____

_____

_____.

5. My spouse loves to be kissed on his/her _____

_____

_____.

---

[25]For a printable version of this quiz, visit https://hotholyhumorous.com/appendix-a/.

6. My spouse's biggest fear is _____

_____

_____ .

7. If we suddenly came into a lot of money, my spouse would want to _____

_____

_____ .

8. My spouse first knew our relationship was headed toward marriage when _____

_____

_____ .

9. My spouse's favorite sexual position is _____

_____

_____ .

10. My spouse's favorite ice cream flavor is _____

_____

_____ .

APPENDIX B
ANATOMY OF A MAN

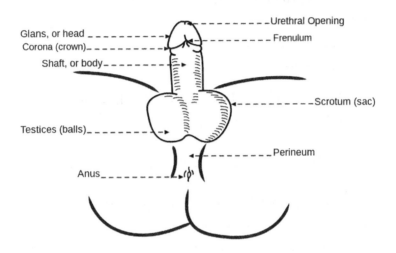

APPENDIX C
ANATOMY OF A WOMAN

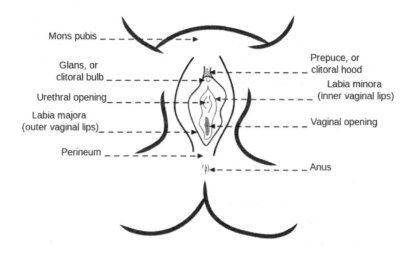

Mons pubis

Glans, or
clitoral bulb

Urethral opening

Labia majora
(outer vaginal lips)

Perineum

Prepuce, or
clitoral hood

Labia minora
(inner vaginal lips)

Vaginal opening

Anus

APPENDIX D
WHAT'S IN THE WAY OF YES?

Following is a list reasons why you have said or would say no to sex at a given time. Check which ones apply to you. Then follow up below answering what, if anything, you could do to minimize or work around each issue. Sometimes the answer will still need to be "not now, later," but you may be able to address more than you initially thought.[26]

Fatigue/sleepiness.
Anger/resentment.
Work or household stress.
Sick or not feeling well.
Busyness/not enough time.
Poor timing.
Menstruation.
Body just not cooperating.
Not in the mood.[27]
Performance anxiety.
Don't feel good about my appearance.
Spouse not clean/groomed enough.
Don't enjoy sex as much as I should.
Other:_____.
Other:_____.

---

[26]Find a printable version of this checklist by visiting https://hotholyhumorous.com/appendix-b/.
[27]See "Are You in the Mood?" chapter.

My issue: _____

How we can address it: _____
_____
_____

My issue: _____
_____
_____

How we can address it: _____
_____
_____

My issue: _____
_____
_____

How we can address it: _____
_____
_____

My issue: _____
_____
_____

How we can address it: _____
_____
_____

APPENDIX E
AROUSAL AND ORGASM

What happens when you have sex?

In 1966 sex researchers Masters and Johnson posited a four-phase sex cycle following this sequence: excitement, plateau, orgasm, and resolution. Another version of the four stages is desire (libido), arousal (excitement), orgasm, and resolution.[28] While this formulation is useful in studying people generally, it's less certain at the individual level. For instance, some people don't have an independent desire that shows up before arousal; rather, their sexuality is more responsive to what's happening. And it's possible for one to go back and forth between stages, such as arousal-orgasm-arousal-orgasm before reaching resolution.

What happens physiologically during arousal and climax can be more helpful in understanding how your body is, or should be, responding. Once you know that, you can better figure out how to achieve the goals of pleasure, orgasm, and intimacy in the marriage bed.

What happens for her. As she experiences arousal, whether before or during foreplay, the wife's vaginal walls produce lubrication, and the clitoris, a wish-boned shaped organ, and surrounding tissue swell. Eventually, her inner labia, or vaginal lips, will reach two to three times their normal size. These lips can also change color, tending to be pink to red in women who have not had children and, due to increased blood flow to that area, red to wine color in women who have.

---

[28]https://my.clevelandclinic.org/health/articles/9119-sexual-response-cycle; "Human Sexual Response Cycle"; Wikipedia. November 12, 2018. Accessed November 27, 2018. https://en.wikipedia.org/wiki/Human_sexual_response_cycle.

Her heart begins to pump faster, causing an increase in blood pressure and breathing. Blood flow, triggered by a surge in nitric oxide, can produce a body flush and makes nipples more sensitive and erect. Her breasts may also increase in size and display veins more prominently. Her vaginal opening narrows in order to grip the penis more tightly.

Her body releases both adrenalin, which increases feelings of exertion and excitement, and dopamine, a neurotransmitter that creates a sense of pleasure and reward.

As she reaches climax, her clitoral bulb, which sticks out at the top of the vulva, becomes more swollen and sensitive, and vaginal walls begin to contract. Her breathing and heart rate speed up, as the autonomic nervous system responds to excitement. Other muscles in her body tense up as well, such as her thighs.

Vaginal contractions can be brief with three to five spasms or longer for intense orgasms with up to fifteen spasms. During this stage, the wife also receives more dopamine as well as a rush of oxytocin. Oxytocin is a chemical that creates a feeling of intimacy and also wipes out the stress hormone cortisol—thus leaving her feeling bonded and relaxed.

Most of the time, a woman does not ejaculate during orgasm, but contact with her Skene's glands can cause a rush of fluid that is or isn't timed with the contractions of an orgasm.

Following orgasm, it takes a few minutes for her body and its parts to return to its normal, everyday pace and size. This stage is labeled resolution.[29]

What happens for him.

Believe it or not, erection begins with relaxation. When aroused by mental or sensory stimulation, two internal

---

[29]Gould, Hallie. 2018. "This Is What Happens to Your Brain When You Have Sex." TheThirty. The Thirty. April 3, 2018. https://thethirty.byrdie.com/what-happens-during-sex/slide2; "How Sex Affects Your Brain." Health.com. Accessed November 27, 2018. https://www.health.com/sex/8-ways-sex-affects-your-brain.

chambers that run the length of penis, the corpora cavernosa, relax—allowing blood to flow into the vessels and fill the open spaces. A surrounding membrane, the tunica albuginea, then traps the blood inside, and the penis becomes erect.

Meanwhile, the scrotum tightens, bringing the testicles closer to the body. The head of the penis becomes wider, and the testicles grow in size. Blood pressure and heart rate increase, and he may feel a warm sensation around the perineum, the length of tissue between penis and anus.

Friction against the glans penis (the head), and particularly the frenulum, a stretchy bit of tissue bridging the head and shift on the underside, creates tension and builds excitement. Internally, the tubes that run from penis to testes contract to push sperm to the base of the penis, and the prostate gland and seminal vesicles release secretions to make semen. As he moves towards orgasm, his thighs and buttocks tighten. Breathing quickens, and the muscles then pulse contractions to force semen out through the penis in up to five spurts.

During sex and orgasm, husbands also receive a wash of dopamine and oxytocin, providing a sense of reward and intimacy. Researchers have also suggested that oxytocin assists him in maintaining an erection and ejaculation.[30]

---

[30]"Erection & Ejaculation." Cleveland Clinic. Accessed November 27, 2018. https://my.clevelandclinic.org/health/articles/10036-erection-ejaculation-how-it-occurs; Kennard, Jerry. "How Men Experience Arousal and What Can Interfere With It." Verywell Health. Accessed November 27, 2018. https://www.verywellhealth.com/sexual-arousal-2329083; "What Happens to Your Body When You Make Love." Daily Mail Online. July 31, 2003. Accessed November 27, 2018. https://www.dailymail.co.uk/femail/article-34841/What-happens-body-make-love.html; Filippi, S., L. Vignozzi, G. B. Vannelli, F. Ledda, G. Forti, and M. Maggi. "Role of Oxytocin in the Ejaculatory Process." Current Neurology and Neuroscience Reports. Accessed November 27, 2018. https://www.ncbi.nlm.nih.gov/pubmed/12834028.

But do we feel aroused?

While you can see physiological effects—such as lubrication and erection—and know biological processes are occurring inside, what matters most is your experience of arousal. Spouses who are more in tune with their body's responses often become more excited internally and experience greater pleasure.

Arousal and pleasure are also linked to how we feel about the marriage relationship itself, both overall and in the moment. Intimacy is created both inside and outside the bedroom. So if your spouse is really turning you on, but you feel distanced from them, sex simply won't feel as good as it could.

Experiencing inhibitions can also limit your pleasure. Worrying about performance, pregnancy, or a sexually transmitted infection can separate you from feelings of arousal. Note that women in particular are more prone to feeling a disconnect between their physiological arousal and experience of pleasure.[31]

If everything is clicking just right with your body, but you still aren't feeling that great, consider what could be happening. Does your relationship need healing? Are other worries getting in the way? Do you need to focus more on the sensations your body is experiencing?

And if your body is not responding as it should, see a doctor or consult a counselor or read my book *Hot, Holy, and Humorous: Sex in Marriage by God's Design* for specific tips on improving sexual intimacy. Teach one another what feels good to you and what helps you climax. God's desire for your marriage bed is absolutely clear in this particular: you should both enjoy being there.

---

[31]Benson, Etienne. "The Science of Sexual Arousal." American Psychological Association. April 2003. Accessed November 27, 2018. https://www.apa.org/monitor/apr03/arousal.aspx.

APPENDIX F
TALKING TO YOUR KIDS ABOUT SEX

Have you had The Talk with your kids?

People sometimes ask this question, and too often parents then presume they need to explain the birds and bees just once.

But how many times have you told your children to do something one single time and they consistently followed your instructions thereafter? I suspect your answer is never. If anything, you have to remind them over and over and over, until your hair goes gray or falls out completely.

Likewise, you must have an ongoing conversation with your children about sex with factual information, values commentary, and God's plan laid out. Be willing to discuss the subject whenever it naturally arises or whenever you need to bring it up. Expect to have several discussions on this topic if you want to pass on a godly view of sexuality.

How do you have an ongoing discussion with your kids about sex? Do you bring it up at the dinner table, as in "Hey, John and Jane, while you eat your chicken and green beans, let's go over female anatomy and erogenous zones"? Awkward. Following are a few tips instead.

Become your child's sexpert. Establish yourself as the go-to person when your children have questions. Be ready to answer with knowledge and confidence. If you don't demonstrate that you know the deal about sex, children assume other resources are more reliable.

That is, if you are silent or clumsy about the subject of sexuality, they might figure it's because you don't know anything about it. That does not mean that everyone who has something to say knows something; plenty of people spout off ignorantly on various topics. But if you say nothing to counter wrong messages and your kid hears them day in and day out, who do you think they will listen to?

Look for opportunities. If you're watching a television show or movie that conveys sexuality or relationships in a way that doesn't agree with your standards, say so. You don't have to make a huge deal about it. However, if a couple is sleeping together before marriage, pipe in with something like, "That's not a good way to start a relationship." If there is a scantily dressed female oozing sensuality on the screen, ask "Why do you think she's dressed like that?" Listen to what your kids say, and then talk about respecting yourself with modesty. If a song has questionable lyrics, inquire what your child thinks the song means. Discuss underlying assumptions that the world makes about sexuality with your child and whether this is God's plan.

Admit you have sex with your spouse. Please do not draw a diagram or reveal details, but it's healthy for children to understand that mommy and daddy having sex within marriage is a blessing from God. When children perceive a healthy representation of sex in their own home—a committed, married couple engaging in intimacy—they are more likely to want, and wait for, such a relationship themselves.

One way you can share that you are physically intimate without revealing too much is to stress that you and your spouse need alone time in your bedroom. As they age, children will figure out what some of that entails and won't inquire further. But they will be aware, and that positive influence remains.

Ask questions. Believe me, your kid does not want to hear you rant on and on for 45 minutes about the pitfalls of premarital sex or the perils of sexually transmitted infections. If every sex talk feels like a college hall lecture, your child may be nodding as you speak, but he's mentally plotting his strategy for conquering the next level of his video game.

You need to have a conversation, which means two people talking, or more if other family members are involved. Ask what your children know and what they want to know. Ask what they think about the world's approach to sexuality. Ask what strategies they have to stay sexually pure until marriage. Listen and then respond.

Avail yourself of quality resources. There are some great resources for teaching your children about sex. Read my posts on talking to your children about sex, and look for books and resources online and in your local Christian bookstore.

You don't have to look them in the eye. As kids get older and experience intense sexual feelings, they may want to talk but are embarrassed. This is one of those times when "Look me in the eye" need not apply. Your child might be better able to absorb the message if eye contact is not required.

You can text back and forth. You can chat in the car on the way to school while your eyes are on the road and not available to glare at your child. You can shoot baskets, play video games, or do crafts at the table and have great talks with your kids.

Relax. You don't have to get everything right to be a godly influence to your kids. You don't have to know everything; you can offer to look things up together. You don't have to defend your less-than-perfect history; you can explain, "I didn't do it right, but I wish I had and I want the best for you." You can blush when you say penis and vagina; you still get credit for teaching your kids the right names.

Thank God parenthood doesn't demand perfection! Being present is far more important to kids than being perfect. So relax. Do your best. Then pray and let God do His part.

GET BONUS CONVERSATIONS

Want more tips for your marriage bed? Sign up for my newsletter! And when you sign up, I'll send you two bonus conversations on Sexual Fantasies and Vacations & Holidays.

Just head to https://hotholyhumorous.com/subscribe/ and share a few bits of information to get on my subscription list. Thanks!

Note: I will never sell or distribute your information to third parties.

ACKNOWLEDGMENTS

Before I became an author, I never read the Acknowledgments. Now I read them in every book, without fail, because I understand writing a book is not a lone endeavor.

So thank you to my three podcast partners, Bonny Burns, Chris Taylor, and Gaye Christmus, for their ongoing support in both professional and "besties" ways. Thanks to Jessica McCleese and Brad Alrich for their expertise on sensate focus therapy and working with a counselor. Thanks to Dan and Emily Purcell, for lighting a (gentle) fire under me to get this book finished. And a special note of gratitude to Brent Trahan for providing the wonderful anatomy illustrations.

To my husband, of course, I owe many thanks. He hears about the books I write far more than anyone else, including my expressions of concern, excitement, and frustration. He remains my anchor.

And always and ever, thank you to my Heavenly Father, whom I question at times only in choosing *me* to write and speak on the topic of Christian sexuality since I often feel out of my league. Yet He keeps calling me to speak up, and so I do.

OTHER BOOKS BY J. PARKER

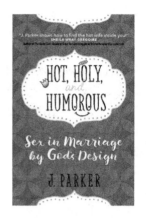

Do you want to be a hottie in the bedroom without sacrificing holiness? How can you make the most of God's gift of sexual intimacy in marriage? Wrongful thinking and behaviors regarding sex permeate our culture. Christians need to reclaim sexuality and enjoy it in the way God intended.

God does not shy away from the subject of sex. The Bible shows a better way in every area—including the marital bedroom.

In *Hot, Holy, and Humorous*, author J. Parker gives candid advice for wives from a foundation of faith with a splash of humor.

This book can boost your sex savvy and improve your marital intimacy. And guess what? With God's perfect design, you and your spouse can enjoy the most amazing sex!

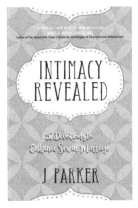

What does the Bible say about sexual intimacy?

Quite a lot actually. From marriage-specific scriptures to biblical principles, *Intimacy Revealed: 52 Devotions to Enhance Sex in Marriage* guides Christian wives through weekly devotions that shed light on God's gift of marital sex.

Each week includes a Bible passage, application, questions, and a prayer. These short devotions will deepen your understanding of God's design of sexuality and encourage you toward a holier, happier, and hotter marriage.

Behind Closed Doors is a collection of five inspirational short stories addressing marriage and sexual intimacy.

ABOUT THE AUTHOR

J. Parker is Christian author and speaker who blogs at Hot, Holy & Humorous and uses a biblical perspective and a blunt sense of humor to foster godly sexuality. Married for 26 years, J. has fondly nicknamed her logical husband "Spock," has two grown sons, and lives in the great state of Texas. She holds a master's degree in counseling, yet it's her personal story of redemption that fuels her passion for passion.

Check out her blog at www.hotholyhumorous.com or follow her on Twitter at @hotholyhumorous, Facebook at HotHolyHumorous, or Pinterest at hotholyhumorous.

61145861R00118